"This moving and inspirational resource is an encouragement to those seeking interfaith understanding. At a time when we often hear only of negativity coming out of Jerusalem, this book introduces us to some lovely individuals in the city who share with us in a personal way their own spiritual practice. It is beautifully balanced between the different faiths, and also between different groups and cultures within those faiths. An emerging theme is the interplay between spirituality and action, and how these cannot be separated in today's world. Challenging questions in each chapter lead readers to prayer, making the resource useful for individuals and study groups alike."

—ANDREW WINGATE, interfaith adviser and author of *Celebrating Difference, Staying Faithful: How to Live in a Multi-faith World*

"As I read *Gateways to the Divine*, I sensed that this is going to be a useful and educative resource for anyone seeking a greater appreciation of the diversity of religious experience today. This is an excellent and unusual book in the way it brings together historic resources and contemporary unheard voices in the search for authentic spirituality. In today's polarized and divided world, this resource breaks barriers and literally opens up gateways of fresh encounter and understanding. It calls us to attentive listening to the Other."

—MICHAEL LEWIS, Archbishop of Province of Jerusalem and the Middle East; Bishop of Cyprus and the Gulf

"This profound book takes the reader deep into the center and the soul of the holy city of Jerusalem. It goes far beneath the surface of things and will enrich all those who delve into the riches. The description of the city which the author knows so well will resonate with those who have visited and will enchant those who have not known its treasures and its complexities. We are drawn into fresh encounters with diverse spiritual traditions which will help build interfaith relationships, whatever our context."

—RICHARD SEWELL, Dean of St. George's College, Jerusalem

Canon Mayes provides what only a person who has walked through these gates and lived with the people of Jerusalem can do for us: share and then reflect upon insights of the faithful 'living stones' from Islam, Judaism and Christianity. As they follow their faith journeys day by day, a multi-faceted context opens before us, weaving together biblical, historical and spiritual insight. A simply excellent resource to lead the reader toward deeper understanding, not just of Jerusalem and her people, but of their own faith journey, too.

—CANON ROBERT D. EDMUNDS, Middle East Partnership Officer, Episcopal Church USA

Gateways to the Divine

Gateways to the Divine

TRANSFORMATIVE PATHWAYS OF PRAYER
FROM THE HOLY CITY OF JERUSALEM

Andrew D. Mayes

CASCADE *Books* · Eugene, Oregon

GATEWAYS TO THE DIVINE
Transformative Pathways of Prayer from the Holy City of Jerusalem

Cascade Books
An Imprint of Wipf and Stock Publishers
199 W. 8th Ave., Suite 3
Eugene, OR 97401

www.wipfandstock.com

PAPERBACK ISBN: 978-1-7252-6041-2
HARDCOVER ISBN: 978-1-7252-6040-5
EBOOK ISBN: 978-1-7252-6042-9

Cataloguing-in-Publication data:

Names: Mayes, Andrew D., author.
Title: Gateways to the divine : transformative pathways of prayer from the
  holy city of Jerusalem / Andrew D. Mayes.
Description: Eugene, OR: Cascade Books, 2020. | Includes bibliographical
  references.
Identifiers: ISBN 978-1-7252-6041-2 (paperback). | ISBN 978-1-7252-6040-
  5 (hardcover). | ISBN 978-1-7252-6042-9 (ebook).
Subjects: LCSH: Jerusalem. | Jerusalem—Travel and description. | Jerusa-
  lem—Geography | Jerusalem—Religious life and customs. | Jerusalem—
  History—21st century. | Prayer. | Self-realization—Religious aspects.
Classification: BV4488 M34 2020 (print). | BV4488 (ebook).

Manufactured in the U.S.A.   OCTOBER 13, 2020

Extracts from Sebastian Brock, *The Luminous Eye: The Spiritual World Vision of Saint Ephrem* (Cistercian Studies Series 124; Kalamazoo: Cistercian, 1992).

Extracts from Eva de Vitray-Meyerovitch, *Rummi and Sufism*, translated by Simone Fattal (Sausalito, CA: Post-Apollo, 1977, 1987).

Extracts from Charles Upton, trans., *Doorkeeper of the Heart: Versions of Rabi'a* (New York: Pir, 1988).

Extracts from Paul Smith, trans. *The Book of Baba Farid* (Campbells Creek, Victoria, Australia: New Humanity, 2012).

Extracts from Deepak Chopra, trans., *The Love Poems of Rumi* (London: Rider, 1998).

Extracts from Jonathan Star, trans., *Rumi: In the Arms of the Beloved* (New York: Tarcher, 1997).

Extracts from Regis J. Armstrong et al, trans. *Francis of Assisi: The Saint- Early Documents* (New York: New City Press 1999).

The author is deeply grateful to all those interviewed, for their generosity of spirit, their honesty, and their openheartedness.

All of the photographs are courtesy of the author.

Contents

Photographs

Introduction

Crossing the Threshold

Enter his gates with thanksgiving,
and his courts with praise.
Give thanks to him, bless his name. (Ps 100:4)

STEP ACROSS THE THRESHOLD and enter another spiritual world!
The gates of the Holy City of Jerusalem beckon us to become pilgrims ready to explore diverse worlds of prayer. Each is an entry
point into a different world spirituality. A transformative journey
opens up before us as we encounter ancient yet fresh pathways of
prayer, triggering both questions and resonances, inviting us to
reconsider and expand our present practice of prayer.

Each gateway leads us to a different expression of prayer and
opens before us a spiritual practice that we may not have encountered before. To cross a threshold always involves a risk, as we
leave behind our status quo and routines, exposing ourselves to
unfamiliar, challenging ways that might change the very way we
pray and relate to God. The city gates of Jerusalem lure us in, each
summoning us to discover another world. Each draws the pilgrim
soul to its unique challenges and blessings.

Thirty short interviews with contemporary Jerusalemite
practitioners of their respective traditions enable us to discover firsthand how their spirituality impacts their lives. The

conversationalists recorded here—from the impoverished peasant in the gutter to the patriarch on his throne—represent a kaleidoscope of spiritual traditions, a mosaic of people. Chapters include a short extract from classic spiritual writers of each tradition, so we can engage firsthand with their treasures.

Historical and Contemporary Meeting Points

In all places on earth, gates are poignant symbols of discovery and interaction. From the beginning, the gates of Jerusalem have been places of significant encounter. David, first Israelite king in Jerusalem, met with his people there: "Then the king got up and took his seat in the gate. The troops were all told, 'See, the king is sitting in the gate'; and all the troops came before the king" (2 Sam 19:8). The gate is a place for socializing and meeting others, so the psalmist observes: "I am the subject of gossip for those who sit in the gate" (Ps 69:12). It is a place for celebration: "I may recount all your praises, and, in the gates of daughter Zion, rejoice in your deliverance" (Ps 9:14). For Amos, the gate is to be place of honesty and justice: "They hate the one who reproves in the gate, and they abhor the one who speaks the truth . . . they push aside the needy in the gate. Hate evil and love good, and establish justice in the gate; it may be that the Lord, the God of hosts, will be gracious" (Amos 5:10, 12, 15).

Today's pilgrim to the holy city encounters the sixteenth-century crenulated battlements encircling the city, built by Suleiman the Magnificent, white stone aglow in bright sunshine. The walls of Jerusalem, originating in the fear of attack and the imperative to close the community off protectively, have been destroyed and rebuilt eighteen times throughout history. A Jebusite wall, revealed by archaeology, testifies to Jerusalem's early history: David encountered this in his initial attack in about 1000 BCE (2 Sam 5). Three hundred years later, Hezekiah strengthened the city's defenses in the face of the Assyrian threat: his massive Broad Wall, eight meters high and eight meters thick, has come to the light of day once again in recent excavations in the Jewish quarter. Nehemiah's mission in the sixth century BCE was to rebuild the walls after their destruction by the Babylonians, and he gives us a vivid account (Neh 4–6). In 70 CE the Romans under Titus besieged the city that had come under the control of Jewish zealots. Hadrian rebuilt the walls when remodeling the city as Aelia Capitolina in 135, and his forum is still to be seen beneath Damascus Gate. The walls have seen a succession of attacks: by the Crusaders in 1099 and Saladin in 1187; General Allenby initiated the British Mandate in 1921 by claiming control of the bulwarks, and after bitter fighting in June 1967, Israeli snipers scaled the parapets to seize charge of them.

But punctuating the walls are seven great city gates that bid us cross their thresholds into a different world. They not only open the wonder of different quarters in the Holy City but also lead us to very different spiritual worlds as well.

Origins of This Book

As an Anglican Franciscan (a member of the Third Order of the Society of Saint Francis) I am committed to its principle: "The Order sets out, in the name of Christ, to break down barriers between people . . . Our chief object is to reflect that openness to all which was characteristic of Jesus."[1] Living in Jerusalem at Saint George's College Jerusalem as Course Director, I wondered how I might somehow fulfil such a challenge. I realized that it must begin with listening and the avoidance of superficiality, so I set out to initiate conversations with people—first those who actually live on the Way of the Cross today, the Via Dolorosa, and later with practitioners or disciples of different faith traditions represented in the Holy City, a holy city paradoxically riven with bitter divisions and fractures. I was struck by the fact that not only were people prepared to share their stories and spiritual experience, but they actually appreciated the chance to really be listened to! I was also privileged to lead a small, intimate interfaith gathering at Saint

---

1. Third Order Society of St. Francis, "The Principles."

George's Cathedral on behalf of the Anglican Diocese of Jerusalem, where two or three representatives from the Jewish, Islamic and Christian traditions met monthly to listen to one another's scriptures and to listen "with the heart." Subsequently working in the Diocese of Chichester as Diocesan Spirituality Adviser, and fulfilling a similar role in the Diocese of Cyprus and the Gulf, and on return visits to Jerusalem as associate professor, I began to see how I could carry on this privileged task. Such exchanges always have the potential to shift perceptions and open up new doors of understanding—the aim of this book.

Outline

The Gate of Mercy and Gate of Repentance make up the Golden Gate on the eastern side of the Temple Mount—but these are long-sealed and await, according to tradition, the returning Messiah to open them. The blocked Golden Gate calls us to examine our openness to encountering religious traditions other than our own. The opening chapter beckons us to leave our comfort zone, dismantle any barriers, and to reflect on the challenge of unblocking any resistance we may have to encountering other spiritual worlds. So we are ready to step out on a journey of discovery as the open gates of Jerusalem summon us. In this introduction, as in all the following chapters, there is a suggested prayer exercise and questions for individual or group reflection, with suggestions for further reading.

The next four chapters usher us into contrasting spiritual worlds, by way of five elements:

1. Invitation: stepping across the gateway, answering the alluring summons, crossing threshold to another spiritual world

2. Encounter: describing a spirituality practice and featuring interviews about how people pray

3. Discovery: examining key themes of the tradition, taking a look at significant spiritual writers

4. Reflection: questions for individual thought or group discussion

5. Experience: prayer exercises enabling us to incorporate something of the learning into our own spiritual practice

First, we enter by way of the southern gate, which leads us immediately to the Jewish tradition and the spirituality of the Kabbalah as practiced by the Hasidic Jews worshiping at the Western Wall. We will meet with Rabbi Mendel as he unpacks for us the way this tradition shapes and reshapes daily life. Kabbalah mystic Cordovero (from the sixteenth century) introduces us to key concepts; we learn too from Israel Ben Eliezer (from the eighteenth century) and Isaac Luria (again from the sixteenth century) and engage with the idea of *tikkun,* repairing the world.

Next we allow the Zion Gate to lead us into the heart of Armenian spirituality, introduced to us by Father Emmanuel, and the treasures of Syriac spirituality as shared by Sister Jostina and Father Shem'on. Our teachers are Armenian mystics Gregory of Narek (from the tenth century) and Nersēs Shnorhali (from the eleventh century) and Syriac writers Ephrem (from the fourth century) and Isaac the Syrian (from the seventh century).

The New Gate leads us into conversations with the superior of the Franciscans in the Holy Sepulcher and with the Greek patriarch of Jerusalem. We learn about Saint Francis's spirituality of the Cross, while one of the greatest mystics of the Eastern Church, Symeon the New Theologian (from the tenth century), leads us into a spirituality of Divine Light.

Herod's Gate entices us into the world of the Sufis as we meet with Sheikh Ahram, overseer of Islamic holy places in Jerusalem, and with Hala, widow of the great Jerusalemite interfaith pioneer Sheikh Abdul Aziz Bukhari. Three Sufi mystics guide us into their world: Raba'a (from the eighth century), Baba Farid (from the twelfth century) and Rumi (from the thirteenth century).

The Lion Gate takes us along the Via Dolorosa, the Way of the Cross, as we meet its present-day residents and engage with their hopes, heartaches, and fears. We talk with Israeli yeshiva students,

Palestinian Christians and Muslims, with those who work with children and young people today on the Via Dolorosa. Suggestions are offered for praying a contemporary Way of the Cross.

As we descend a stunning flight of steps to the magnificent Damascus Gate, a common entry point shared by the faithful from all the religions, it invites us to identify common themes in the contrasting spiritualities. We compare and contrast approaches to such themes as naming the Divine (the invocation of divine names); divinization within mortality; the place of the heart; the role of the body in prayer practices; and the interrelationship between the mystical and prophetic, the inner life and the outer life in the world.

Finally, the wide and noble Jaffa Gate opens the city to the west. The Jaffa Gate catapults us back into the world we inhabit, leading as it does to port and airport from which pilgrims return to their home contexts renewed and transformed. Named also the Gate of the Friend because it points to Abraham's city of Hebron, the Jaffa Gate reminds us that Abraham, father of the monotheistic religions, teaches us how to cultivate an utter openness to the divine, how to develop a pilgrim heart, how to practice hospitality to the Other, and how to take risks and foster interfaith friendships. These issues lead us from the encounters in this book to the interfaith opportunities and challenges that we face in our own setting and context.

This is a resource for individuals or groups. It would make an unusual and stimulating Lent course, for example,[2] but can be used at any time of year by a study group or interfaith group. Participants can be encouraged to keep a "travel diary" or journal, to note reactions and responses to the journey or to reflect on shifting perceptions. Such material can perhaps be shared with a "soul friend" or spiritual director. Noticing what excites or inspires you, what fills you with caution, what resistance or openness you feel—all this tells you about your own spiritual journey right now.

2. If used for a Lent course, the introduction could be combined with the first session and the Jaffa Gate with chapter 7, making six sessions.

Doors of Opportunity

The opening of doors is a powerful biblical image. The Risen Lord calls out to us: "Listen! I am standing at the door, knocking; if you hear my voice and open the door, I will come in to you and eat with you, and you with me" (Rev 3:20). In his narrative of the early church, Luke describes the pushing back of doors: "When they arrived, they called the church together and related all that God had done with them, and how he had opened a door of faith for the Gentiles" (Acts 14:27). Paul too develops the metaphor of the open door: "A wide door for effective work has opened to me, and there are many adversaries" (1 Cor 16:19). He relates: "When I came to Troas to proclaim the good news of Christ, a door was opened for me in the Lord" (2 Cor 2:12). He asks: "Pray for us as well that God will open to us a door for the word, that we may declare the mystery of Christ, for which I am in prison" (Col 4:3).

Fling Wide the Gates

Psalm 87 reminds us that Jerusalem is a universal wellspring of faith, and from it we can trace many diverse life-giving traditions of spirituality: "The source of my life springs from Jerusalem!" (Ps 87:7, NLT):

> On the holy mount stands the city he founded;
>> the LORD loves the gates of Zion
>> more than all the dwellings of Jacob.
> Glorious things are spoken of you,
>> O city of God.
> Among those who know me I mention Rahab and Babylon;
>> Philistia too, and Tyre, with Ethiopia—
>> "This one was born there," they say.
> And of Zion it shall be said,
>> "This one and that one were born in it";
>> for the Most High himself will establish it.

The LORD records, as he registers the peoples,
"This one was born there."
Singers and dancers alike say,
"All my springs are in you." (Ps 87:1–7)

The Gates of Zion, beloved of God, summon us to fresh adventures of faith, new discoveries of spirituality. We echo Psalm 122:

I was glad when they said to me,
"Let us go to the house of the LORD!"
Our feet are standing
within your gates, O Jerusalem.
Jerusalem—built as a city
that is bound firmly together.
To it the tribes go up,
the tribes of the LORD . . .
Pray for the peace of Jerusalem:
"May they prosper who love you.
Peace be within your walls,
and security within your towers."
For the sake of my relatives and friends
I will say, "Peace be within you."
For the sake of the house of the LORD our God,
I will seek your good.

With Psalm 24 we realize the gates symbolize access to the Divine, and access for the Divine:

Fling wide the gates,
open the ancient doors,
and the great king will come in.
Who is this great king?
He is the LORD, strong and mighty,
the LORD, victorious in battle.
Fling wide the gates,
open the ancient doors,
and the great king will come in. (Ps 24:7–9, GNT)

This book is an invitation to witness the glory and grace of God, as it is discovered in astonishingly diverse ways today.

FIGURE 1

At the Golden Gate

Identifying Resistances

THE GOLDEN GATE, DOUBLE-ARCHED and facing east, radiates a honey-colored hue as the sun rises over the Mount of Olives and casts its first rays of light on it at each dawn. It is famous throughout the world, because the iconic golden Dome of the Rock can be seen rising above it: this is the most widely recognized view of Jerusalem. But the gate is blocked. Access is denied. Situated above the site of the ancient Shushan Gate, the eastern entry point to the Temple Mount, by which Jesus entered the city on Palm Sunday, it was walled up in the eighth century by Muslim authorities out of fear, to prevent Jews entering the former Temple area. After being reopened in 1102 by the Crusaders, it was resealed by Saladin after he regained Jerusalem in 1187. The Ottoman Sultan Suleiman the Magnificent strengthened the barrier in 1541 when he built the city walls, and it has stayed closed up to the present day.

This gate stands as both a caution and invitation. It calls us, at the outset of this exploration, to name and remove the blockages, barriers, prejudices, and fears that hold us back from crossing the threshold into other faith worlds. The sealed Golden Gate represents defensiveness, exclusion, an inability to welcome or encounter the Other. It might symbolize for us our hesitations or anxieties as we face the prospect of leaving the familiar behind.

But also represents abiding hope. For Muslims, the gate is referred to as Bab al-Dhahabi or Bab al-Zahabi (meaning "Golden Gate" or "Gate of Eternal Life"). Muslims also place religious significance at this location, as some believe that this is the site of Allah's final judgment and the site of future resurrection. Muslims call its double doors "the gate of mercy" and "the gate of penance."

For the Jewish people, the gate symbolizes undying expectations. The prophet Ezekiel had related:

> Then he brought me to the gate, the gate facing east. And there, the glory of the God of Israel was coming from the east; the sound was like the sound of mighty waters; and the earth shone with his glory . . . As the glory of the LORD entered the temple by the gate facing east, the spirit lifted me up, and brought me into the inner court; and the glory of the LORD filled the temple. (43:1–5)

In Jewish tradition this is the gate through which the Anointed One, the Messiah, will enter Jerusalem. Looking across the Kidron Valley to the Mount of Olives, this gate has come to represent humanity's longing for redemption.

Only God can open this door. But in preparation and anticipation, we can start to remove the blockages in our own soul that impede the advent of the Divine. We need courage to cross new thresholds of understanding, and to help dismantle walls of misunderstanding where they exist. This requires pilgrim-readers to examine their *own* walls and barricades. It requires of pilgrims a readiness to lower the self-protective barriers and armory that we unconsciously erect around ourselves to guard ourselves from getting too close to what might challenge us. We need the grace to first recognize, then chip away at, our own walls and defenses. This is a basic requirement for pilgrims—to be ready for some measure of brokenness and honesty, as we expose our hearts and minds to new insights, new ways of seeing things, different cultures. This is the essential risk of learning—a preparedness to change!

But the dismantling of walls requires both human effort and divine grace. We must not only be prepared for hard work in changing our attitudes—we must open ourselves afresh to the grace of Christ. He is the one who breaks down walls and opens up new possibilities. He is the one who makes breakthroughs possible. He calls himself "the gate" (John 10:9). At the start of his ministry and at the end of it, what is formerly locked and closed is now opened up. At his baptism he sees the walls of heaven itself torn apart (Mark 1:10). At his death the heavy curtain separating the temple's Holy of Holies from the people, a persistent barrier between humans and God, is likewise ripped asunder, from top to bottom (Mark 15:38). On Easter Day, when the disciples hide themselves away and the doors "were locked for fear," the Risen Christ is not impeded by walls of anxiety: he breaks through and greets his people with the words: "Peace be with you!" (John 20:19). As the Letter to the Ephesians puts it, "He has broken down the dividing wall, the hostility between us . . . through the cross" (2:14, 16).

Looking at the mighty walls of Jerusalem, Jesus foresees their demolition: "You're impressed by this grandiose architecture? There's not a stone in the whole works that is not going to end up in a heap of rubble!" (Mark 13:2, *The Message*).

You've Only Just Begun . . .

Where can we look to find clues that will help us shape a spirituality that inspires openness to the Divine rather than defensive wall-building? Gregory of Nyssa (335–395), one of the outstanding theologians of the Eastern Church, who lived in Cappadocia in the fourth century, communicated an exciting vision of the spiritual life as continually evolving and progressing. His key text was the resolve of Paul: "Forgetting what lies behind, and straining forward to what lies ahead, I press on toward the goal, for the prize of the upward call of God in Christ Jesus" (Phil 3:13–14). Here Paul is saying that there is no room for self-satisfaction in the Christian life. We should never stand still, but continually stretch ourselves towards the "upward call."

Gregory invites us to accept the vocation of adventurers, in which we are beckoned to keep on growing. Gregory urges us to break free from any way of life that seems deterministic and predictable; to jump off the treadmill of dull routine which traps us into going around in circles. Rather he encourages us to discover our full potential in Christ: "the finest aspect of our mutability is the possibility of growth in good . . . let us change in such a way that we may constantly evolve towards what is better, being transformed from glory into glory, and thus always improving and ever becoming more perfect by daily growth."[1] For Gregory, each stage we reach in the spiritual journey is but a beginning, not an end. We can never say we have arrived. As the Letter to the Hebrews puts it, "Let us lay aside every weight, and sin which clings so closely, and let us run with perseverance the race that is set before us, looking to Jesus the pioneer and perfecter of our faith" (12:1–2). In Gregory's eyes, the greatest sin is that of complacency, of resting on our laurels. We are not to allow ourselves to become too content with where we are spiritually. We are not to rest in our achievements in a spirit of self-congratulation. God ever calls us to the next stage of our development. Every point of arrival is to be a springboard that catapults us into another adventure! We must keep moving.

This, however, requires of us great determination and resolve. We need to foster an unending sense of yearning and desire to grow in faith. For Gregory, it is a question of a partnership between human effort and divine help. It is the Holy Spirit who can transform our life into an adventure of moving further into the mystery of God. The Spirit enables us to participate in the divine life itself, which animates, vivifies, and completes human life: "The rich and ungrudging Spirit is always flowing into those accepting grace . . . for those who have taken possession of this gift sincerely, it endures as a co-worker and companion in accordance with the measure of faith."[2] The Holy Spirit helps us reach our full potential and an ever-increasing likeness to God; as Gregory puts it, "the soul having been brought to the full flower of its beauty by the grace of the Spirit."[3] Gregory pictures the Holy Spirit as a Dove

1. Musurillo, ed. and trans., *From Glory to Glory*, 51–52.
2. Gregory of Nyssa, *Ascetical Works*, 129.
3. Gregory of Nyssa, *Ascetical Works*, 130.

4

who not only broods over our life but actually gives us wings to fly, never staying put for long upon the mountain, but ever ascending: "the soul keeps rising higher and higher, stretching with its desire for heavenly things 'to those that are before' as the Apostle tells us, and thus it will always continue to soar ever higher."[4]

Push Open the Door!

Teresa of Avila (1515–1582) challenges us through vivid images to embrace the changes and shifts that can take place in us if we persevere in a questing, venturesome spirit in the journey of prayer. In *The Interior Castle*, depicting the soul as a crystal castle with many rooms, with Christ dwelling at the center, she invites the reader to trace a journey through successive stages in order to reach a state of mystical union:

> I began to think of the soul as if it were a castle made of a single diamond or of very clear crystal, in which there are many rooms, just as in Heaven there are many mansions. Now if we think carefully over this, the soul of the righteous one is nothing but a paradise, in which, as God tells us, He takes His delight. For what do you think a room will be like which is the delight of a King so mighty, so wise, so pure and so full of all that is good? I can find nothing with which to compare the great beauty of a soul and its great capacity . . . (though) the very fact that His majesty says it is made in His image means that we can hardly form any conception of the soul's great dignity and beauty . . .
>
> Let us imagine that this castle contains many mansions, some above, others below, others at each side; and in the center and midst of them all is the chiefest mansion where the most secret things pass between God and the soul.[5]

4. Musurillo, trans. and ed., *From Glory to Glory*, 57.
5. Teresa of Avila (trans. Peers), *Interior Castle*, 1, 2.

The image conveys the beauty and potential of the soul: the door to the castle, and indeed its weaving corridor, is the experience of prayer. Rowan Williams observes:

> If the soul is a home for God, it is a home with an enor-
> mous abundance of rooms, and we shall need to know
> where we are if we are not to be deceived and think we
> have encountered God when we have not . . . the journey
> inward is a journey to the place where God's love meets
> and mingles with the life of the soul, and thus we need to
> keep moving through the rooms until we find the middle
> of what sounds remarkably like a maze . . . We do not
> know where the boundaries are if we never move for-
> ward and walk into them. We need to know what we are
> capable of, positively and negatively.[6]

The first three rooms represent an increasing detachment from the things of the world and a process of deepening repentance and humility. In the first room of self-knowledge, we start to realize that we are made for God. The second room calls us to conquer the pull to turn back to the attractions of the world, so we remain very focused and single-minded in the interior journey. But it is the third room where we most often get stuck. This represents the stability and predictability of endlessly repeated respectable routines and normal disciplines of the religious life, like word-filled prayers. A sign or indicator that the soul is ready to move on from these reveals itself in a holy restlessness or discontent with unfulfilling dutiful praying—a craving for a greater interior freedom and a desire to jump off what may have become the treadmill of religious practice. We discover in our soul a curiosity, not for the novel but for ancient wisdom, tried and tested through the centuries. God places within us a thirst for something *more*. What is important is that we desire fresh intimations of the Divine, that we yearn for more of God.

As Teresa sketches a possible itinerary for us, a significant turning point in the journey comes with entry into the voluminous and spacious fourth room, a place of new discovery which opens

6. Williams, *Teresa of Avila*, 113, 114.

us up to "supernatural prayer": "Supernatural prayer is where God takes over. It is also called infused contemplation, passive prayer, mystical prayer, or infused prayer. All labels, again, mean the same thing. This type of prayer means that God is communicating with the person."[7] Teresa advises: "the important thing is not to think much, but to love much."[8] A letting-go of former restrictive practices of prayer enables a movement from the primacy of ego to the initiative of God.

But there is no need to rest even here: we can go deeper into God if we have the courage to keep moving: the fifth room is a place of liberation where the soul breaks free from its chrysalis or cocoon learns to "fly" in a new freedom. In the sixth, the pilgrim-soul stumbles on a glittering treasury concealed in the inner depths: a storehouse of spiritual gifts. Here Teresa speaks of the soul's betrothal to God, while in the seventh she uses the daring language of mystical marriage to describe union with God as an abiding awareness and permanent consciousness of unity with the indwelling Christ. As Teresa provides a sketch of the spiritual life through the imagery of one room leading to another in a mysterious castle of prayer, the main point is, whatever room of prayer you find yourself in, this room has an enticing gateway or doorway opposite the way in, beckoning you to yet-unexplored reaches of prayer. Don't get stuck in one room. Go on: attempt the next gateway, push the door open, and see where it leads!

This is the challenge of the Golden Gate. It looks beautiful, it is admired, and it has a lovely name.[9] But the fact remains: it remains blocked, shut, closed. In our spiritual venturing, we do not need to stand impassively in front of closed doors or walls, even if they have become something of a comfort or security to us. God calls us to depart from our resignation to routine, from impotency,

---

7. Humphreys, *From Ash to Fire*, 80.

8. Teresa of Avila (trans. Peers), *Interior Castle*, 33.

9. This name links with the Beautiful Gate of Acts 3:2, 10. The term "Golden Gate" derives from the Latin Vulgate version of the Bible: Jerome, translating the New Testament into Latin in the fourth century, changed the Greek *oraia*, meaning "beautiful," into the similar-sounding Latin *aurea*, meaning "golden."

from a fatalistic sense that what our spiritual life is now is what it shall always be. Rather, God invites us to name and confront any barriers to discovery, anything that holds us back. Ps 18:30 invites us to dismantle walls: "With You I will break down barricades; with the help of my God I will scale any wall." That is the ultimate challenge of the Golden Gate. The wonders of the City summon us, and we will not let *anything* get in our way!

The Gate of Repentance: Bigger Heart, Bigger Mind

We noted that one of the doors in the Golden Gate is called the gate of repentance, prompting us to recall Jesus' summons: "The time is fulfilled, and the kingdom of God has come near; repent and believe in the good news." Mark's Gospel gives us these dramatic words as the starting point, the opening lines of Jesus' proclamation (1:15). "Repent!" We usually read this in a moralistic way, as calling us to penitence, but as recent writers have reminded us, it is in fact a summons to an utterly different way of seeing reality.[10] The word is literally *meta*, meaning "beyond" or "large," and *noia*, which translates as "mind." Jesus is calling us to "go beyond the mind" or to "go into the big mind." He is inviting us to a fresh way of seeing things, a new consciousness. He is demanding that we let go our former defensive mindsets and risk the discovery of a new vision of things.

At the outset of this journey of discovery, let's pray both for a bigger mind and a for bigger heart. As the psalmist (in Ps 119:32) puts it, "enlarge my heart!" (ESV), "expand my understanding" (NLV), "broaden my understanding" (CSB), "help me to understand more" (CEV).

Approaching the temple courts through the original gate, the psalmist prays (in Ps 18:19) for a spaciousness of soul, a greater capacity for the Divine, an expansiveness of mind, and then he rejoices: "He brought me out to wide-open spaces"(CEB); Wycliffe renders this: "he led me out into breadth." We are invited to take

---

10. See Rohr, *Naked Now*; and Bourgeault, *Wisdom Jesus*.

the risk to leave behind restricting, narrow thinking that ties the Divine down into neat boxes, categories and concepts. We realize, perhaps, where we have become constrained, held back, tied down in our thinking about God, or in our practice of prayer.

Risking an Encounter with the Other

Have you ever noticed how many times in the gospels Jesus says: "Let us go over to the other side"? He asks his disciples to leave the security of Capernaum, a conservative, traditional, mainly Jewish town, and to traverse the choppy waters of Galilee to enter enemy territory: the pagan, heathen, Gentile terrain of the Decapolis—Greco-Roman land, shores where unclean demoniacs and Gadarene pigs lurk uncontrolled.

Normally, that is a place to be avoided: to go there would contaminate the devout Jew. But Jesus calls his disciples to quit their safety zone and risk encounter with the Other, with those who are definitely "not us." Significantly, Mark tells us, that Jesus went directly from his encounter with the Syrophoenician woman (Mark 7) to the pagan territories of the Decapolis: "Then he returned from the region of Tyre, and went by way of Sidon towards the Sea of Galilee, in the region of the Decapolis" (Mark 7:31). In Tyre he had met someone who expanded his own consciousness and vision. He was empowered and inspired by his meeting with the Other represented in the Syrophoenician woman to go straight to areas on the very frontier of the Roman Empire: the group of ten cities marked by Greek culture. Jesus led his disciples here that they might discover the Hellenistic way of life so different from Jewish values. Indeed, Jews were often affronted and dismayed by aspects of this foreign world: by the nude wrestling, the gymnasia and the theatres. He wanted them to experience culture shock! Matthew tells us that later Jesus again crossed over to the eastern region beyond the Jordan, and he locates significant encounters and teaching there. The enemy, pagan terrain becomes the land of discovery.

What is entailed in the transition here, as we meet with different worldviews? First, we must be prepared to move. Jesus undertook an exhausting journey across the northern Galilee hills to reach Tyre and Sidon and ventured across the dangerous waters of the Sea of Galilee to reach the region of the Decapolis. We must move, physically or spiritually, in order to seek out the Other, and in the process of relating, we discover that the Other is really part of us. The journey towards the Other becomes the discovery that we are all part of one another. The mindsets that had fenced us off, that had kept us safely apart, dissolve into the astonishing revelation that we belong to one another. I am incomplete without my neighbor. For this transition to take place, we must be prepared to lower our self-protective barriers and be ready to be startled or disturbed, and shaken out of the comfortable patterns of thinking we are accustomed to. Above all, we should be ready to change, daring to see things from an alternative point of view.

The Syrophoenician woman—we never learn her name— teaches us that unexpected sources not only can instruct us but can also be life-transformative and revolutionize our understanding of God's ways. Unexplored territories of prayer now beckon us. We are prompted to engage with spiritual seekers and writers who may act as a stimulus to fresh ways of praying, as a catalyst to attempt different ways of discovering God and the Scriptures. Such writers or figures may be literally foreign to us, and like the Syrophoenician woman, may have the capacity to subvert our thinking, disrupt our cherished patterns of prayer, or interrupt our fixated trains of thought. This is the challenge of the thresholds that await us. We need to be ready to be unnerved, unsettled, and spurred on in our spiritual journey. We should be ready for our existing and inherited mindsets to be challenged. Let's become explorers once again.

Crossing Thresholds

As we traverse the inviting thresholds of the city gates, we encounter the inspiring, unsettling, and energizing concept of liminality.

The *limen* is the threshold, the place of departure, a springboard into a fresh way of doing things. In entering liminal space, we leave behind our former ideals and conventions, the status quo, the ordinary routines, inherited mindsets. We also leave behind our safety zone; we quit our place of security. We step out into a space where we may see things differently, where our worldview might be shattered, where our existing priorities might be turned upside down. We cross a border and go beyond our usual limits. What had been a barrier now becomes a threshold, a stepping-stone into a larger spiritual adventure. The limens of Jerusalem become places of radical unmaking and unlearning—uncomfortable spaces where we're called to be utterly vulnerable to God, and from which we will reenter the world quite changed, even transformed by our encounter of different spiritualities.[11]

In the eleventh century outstanding Muslim scholar and Sufi mystic Abu Hamid Al-Ghazali (1058–1111) lived in a room above the Golden Gate while he wrote his vastly influential work on spirituality titled *The Revival of the Religious Sciences*. He experienced the Gate of Mercy to be a place of conversion and transformation. We might begin the spiritual adventure of this book following his advice: "You may say when you begin an activity: 'Our Lord, give

11. The concept of liminality derives from Arnold van Gennep's 1909 *The Rites of Passage*. He identified three stages in a process of transition: *separation*, a metaphorical death or breaking with past practices and expectations; a *liminal state* where those to be initiated, for example young people into adulthood, face challenges to their sense of identity and a process of re-formation; *aggregation*, or reintegration into the community as a changed person with a sharpened sense of values. Victor Turner took this further in his studies among tribes in Zambia, noticing that the transitional phase was a testing process of undoing and remaking. The place of liminality is a place of ambiguity and confusion as one thought-world is left behind, and things are shaken up before one can reenter society with a different perspective, indeed a different social status. This is the place of "anti-structure": the opposite to the world of normality and of usual structures and roles, the place of status quo, "business as usual." But while it is a place of uncertainty, it is precisely here that the person clarifies his or her sense of identity and purpose. Things are discovered in the liminal zone that can't be found in the routines of normal life. See Turner, *Ritual Process;* Turner and Ross, *Image and Pilgrimage*.

us mercy from You, and prepare for us a right path in our affairs. My Lord, open my breast, and ease my task for me.'"

Questions for Reflection

1. Can you name any obstacles that hinder or threaten to impede your journey towards unfamiliar spiritual worlds, any obstructions of the soul?

2. Can you identify anything in your experience that has the effect of restricting your spiritual progress, maybe constraining, holding you back?

3. Following Teresa's imagery, how would you describe the room of prayer you find yourself in right now, your present experience or default position?

4. To what kind of prayer do you sense you might be summoned? What kind of prayer intrigues you and arouses your curiosity?

5. What are you feeling at the outset of this journey of discovery?

Prayer Exercise

As you reflect on these questions, gently and hopefully repeat the prayer of the psalmist: *"I shall run the way of Your commandments, for You will enlarge my heart"* (Ps 119:32, NASB). Prayerfully ask yourself: How can I identify my own self-protective fences? How prepared am I to lower my defenses as I encounter the Other? In what ways am I being called to dismantle fences and become a reconciler? What is stopping me from becoming the person God wants me to be? Maybe it will help to picture this: assign to a block in the gateway the name of something holding you back from God. See the divine hand prying it out, and as it tumbles to the ground, see how light is shining through the opening in your life, bringing joy. The gateway is opening!

Further Reading

Mayes, Andrew D. *Beyond the Edge: Spiritual Transitions for Adventurous Souls.* London: SPCK, 2013.

FIGURE 2

2

Through the Southern Gate

Discovering Kabbalah

Invitation

THE SOUTHERN GATE (DUNG Gate) leads to the Jewish Quarter and to memories of the Temple. The gate is first mentioned in the biblical narrative by Nehemiah, upon the return from the exile:

> I went out by night by the Valley Gate past the Dragon's Spring and to the Dung Gate, and I inspected the walls of Jerusalem that had been broken down and its gates that had been destroyed by fire.
>
> . . .
>
> Malchijah son of Rechab, ruler of the district of Beth-haccherem, repaired the Dung Gate; he rebuilt it and set up its doors, its bolts, and its bars. (2:13; 3:14)

The account reveals the anxiety lurking behind a defensiveness and fear of attack. Today's Dung Gate is a welcoming entry point, giving direct access to the Western Wall, where Hasidic Jews dance and chant in both penitence and exultation, as they approach the remnant of the Temple through the western wall plaza.[1] This gate invites us to discover their world.

---

1. Arabs call this gate the Mughrabi Gate because prior to 1967 it led to the Moroccan quarter. One hundred eighty-six Moroccan homes were demolished after 1967 to open up a gathering space in front of the Western Wall.

We get carried along by joyous processions: piercing tones from a shofar horn and exuberant drumming compete with ululations from Jewish mothers and aunts as families accompany a young man from the gate to his bar mitzvah ceremony at the Wall, (*kotel* in Hebrew). We pass the sign erected by the chief rabbinate of Israel: "You are approaching the site of the Western Wall, where the Divine Presence always rests." As we get closer, we hear the intensifying sound of the buzzing and humming of prayer, as Jewish men rock jerkily backwards and forwards in the rhythmic movements of their *davening*, following the pulse of the psalms being recited. Men pray alone at the Wall, pressing their forehead against the ancient rocks or extending their hands across its hallowed surface. Soldiers from the Israeli Defense Force stand alongside old men whose sobbing reminds us that this is also called the Wailing Wall, where Jews lament the Romans' destruction of the temple in 70 CE and pray for its rebuilding. If there is a *minyan* or quorum of ten adult males, then a little synagogue (gathering) for corporate prayer is possible anywhere. A separate section is reserved for the women. Petitions written on scraps of paper are squeezed into the gaps between the Herodian blocks that make up the Wall—which is the retaining structure upholding the platform that Herod constructed just prior to the time of Jesus.

We notice the distinctive attire worn by Jewish men. In Jerusalem, Jewish identity reflects the cultures of the Diaspora, with a diversity of communities that originated in many different parts of the world. There are three main groupings: Askenazi Jews, of German or Eastern European descent (making up 80 percent of all Jews worldwide); Sephardic Jews, originating from the Iberian Peninsula; and Mizrahi Jews, or (Middle) Easterners, including those from eastern counties and also from North Africa.

The most visible community is the Haredi or ultra-Orthodox, some of whom are Hasidic, belonging to the revivalist and devotional traditions originating with Israel ben Eliezer (1700–1760). The men identify themselves by their beards and side locks (*peyos*, see Lev 19:27) and their black jackets (*reckel*). Their heads are covered by a black felt hat (*fedora*) or a fur hat (*shtreimel*); like all religious Jews they wear a skullcap or *kippah*. The women cover their hair with a scarf or a wig as it is not to be seen in public. Long fringes or tassels (*tzitzit*) descending from a vest or prayer shawl draped over head and shoulders (*tallit katan*) remind worshipers of the 613 commandments (see Num 15:38). Haredi wear on their forehead the phylactery or *tefillin*, a small box containing words from the Torah, with its leather straps going up the arm (in fulfilment of Deut 6:8).

Encounter

Quite close by, above the ancient Roman market street known as the Cardo, the Chabad-Lubavitch synagogue is a place of welcome for all inquirers. Here forty young men study daily. The building dates from 1847. Rabbi Menachem Mendel of Lubavitch (1789–1865), also known as the Tzemach Tzedek, sought a place of study for Jews leaving Hebron at that time. They appealed to English philanthropist Moses Montefiore: "We have no proper place for prayer and worship, to study Torah. We lack holy books and a proper place to keep them . . . We have nowhere to turn, no one to lean on other than the kindness of *Hashem*, our Father in heaven." Funds from various sources enabled the building of a structure around a central courtyard, and a stairway leads to the upstairs synagogue and library.

As I step into the Chabad House, through its arches on the street, I am greeted warmly by Rabbi Mendel Osdoba, who welcomes me with his kind, long-lashed eyes. We chat in his book-lined study. He wears a black hat and suit—and I notice that under his white shirt he wears the *tallit* prayer shawl with its dripping tassels.[2]

> What is prayer? To pray means literally to ask, beseech. But for me prayer is about connection. It's not about begging, it's about connecting with God. Life without prayer is like a Rolls Royce without an engine!

2. Rabbi Mendel Osdoba, interview by Andrew Mayes in August 2011 at Chabad House.

This place is called Chabad House. *Chabad* means "wisdom, understanding, knowledge." What we try to do is to bring down the lofty ideals of Kabbalah to a popular level, so we can understand. We have to integrate Jewish philosophy into daily life. Spirituality is a way of life. We aim to implement our philosophy throughout all of life, every aspect.

We don't seek mystical experience for itself. We are not after experiences. It's not about angels and bright lights. We seek God himself. Man can bend low and reach up high. We serve God in all places, not just in the synagogue, but all the time. Outside and inside must match—what goes on in the heart and what goes on in the body and the world. Some people say they are spiritual on the inside but secular on the outside. But that is a false division and dichotomy. Even when you are playing soccer you're praying—for a healthy body! Hasidic philosophy teaches us that eating a piece of cake is serving God and can be holy. If we approach the mundane and corporal with the right intention, everything can become holy. Eating with the right attitude takes us closer to God. Food is not gross.

The central Jewish prayer is the prayer of blessing. Jewish spirituality celebrates the goodness of creation: "And God saw that it was good" (Gen 1:12). So we fill our days with *berakhah*, blessing God for his gifts: "Blessed are you, Lord God, King of the universe . . ." By blessing God in everything we lift it to a different level, we elevate it to God. So we have both special times and hours of prayer (morning, afternoon, evening) and also consecrate all of life by prayer. . . .

I always want to tell non-Jewish inquirers about the seven laws of Noah, because they are universal; they are for all humanity: believe in one God, revere the creator of the universe, uphold the sanctity of human life, respect property, honor marriage and family life, respect animals, and take responsibility for human society with a system of justice. We Jews have 613 commandments to attend to: you Gentiles have seven! This is a universal moral code which we can all live out![3]

Chabad House follows the teaching of Rabbi Menachem Mendel Schneerson, who led the Lubavitcher movement for forty-four years. He teaches about the energy within, about the inter-relationship between body and soul: "Leading a meaningful life means being able to pierce the outer, material layer and connect to the energy within . . . Listen when your soul cries out for better nourishment than it is being given; listen to your inner voice that expresses doubt and sadness when you immerse yourself exclusively in material concerns. Trust your inner voices . . . Prayer is the emotional ladder that connects you from below; prayer, not materialism, provides you with a real home, a place within your body where the soul can find peace and perspective."[4]

Discovery

At the center of Jewish daily prayers are the nineteen blessings that make up the *Amidah* (lit. "standing"), which is recited three times daily—morning, afternoon, and evening. This prayer is chanted quietly or whispered, and so is often called "the silent prayer." The early Kabbalists advised that before worshipers begin the *Amidah*, they take three steps backward, and then three steps forward. This movement is observed today, enhancing concentration and stimulating greater focus. The movement forward indicates and symbolizes entry into the Creator's innermost chamber. The worshiper symbolically enters a sacred space in which to encounter God's presence. The three steps recall Moses's entry into prayer on Mount Sinai, passing the darkness, the first cloud, and the second cloud, before he encountered the Divine. Worshipers can also visualize themselves moving into the Holy Land with the first step, then into Jerusalem with the second step, and into the temple with the third step, thus standing on the threshold of the Holy of Holies. After the

3. Rabbi Mendel Osdoba, interview by Andrew Mayes, August 2011 at Chabad House.

4. Jacobson, *Toward a Meaningful Life*, 5, 10, 11.

introductory three steps forward and backward, worshipers stand with feet together to be like the angels in the innermost chamber before God. This rootedness represents a surrender of one's sense of a separate self, and a unity with the Divine. Facing toward Jerusalem, each person concentrates on his or her prayers, often looking inside a prayerbook. Many sway gently, uttering words that only they and their Creator can hear.

The nineteen blessings of the *Amidah* fall into three sections: praising God, making petition, and thanking God. Opening praises orient one towards the providence and holiness of God. Petitions seek intellectual enlightenment and wisdom, and a state of closeness with God. They seek forgiveness and healing, and delivery from pain and strife. Concluding thanksgivings include a longing for the restoration of the temple, for peace and goodness in the world.[5]

Welcoming the Divine

The literal meaning of the word *Kabbalah* is "that which is received." It invites us to become receptive and ready to open ourselves to surprising aspects of the Divine. Let's identify key concepts in Kabbalah with the help of Rabbi Moshe Cordovero (1522–1570), who lived alongside Isaac Luria (1532–1572), the leader of this spiritual renaissance in Safed in the Galilee hills, where it developed after the Jewish mystics were expelled from Spain. In a key passage from *The Palm Tree of Devorah*, Cordovero employs seven key concepts:

Kavanah—the true intention of the heart and mind in prayer—both emotional and intellectual—involving a focused concentration and devotion

Mechaven—a person with this orientation and awareness of the Divine, maintaining a mystic approach to every word used in prayer

5. See Center for Jewish Spirituality, "Amidah" (http://iyyun.com/teachings/amidah-the-silent-prayer/).

Devekut—mystical cleaving to God, seeking attachment and connection with the Divine

Shechinah—the dwelling or settling of the divine presence, understood in Kabbalah as the feminine aspect of Divinity

The Tetragrammaton—the four letters representing the divine name YHWH, so holy that they cannot be uttered; hence the Divine is designated in English as G-d

atzmut—the Infinite Light or mysterious divine essence (an alternative is *Ein Sof*, meaning "no end" or Infinite)

Sefirot/sefirah (sing,)—emanations from God, the divine attributes radiating out to the world. These express ten dimensions of the inner being of God, elements that compose the consciousness of God. They represent aspects of the divine energy that flows to the world and are depicted in the central Kabbalah mystic symbol, the Tree of Life:

CROWN
(mystery of the Infinite)
UNDERSTANDING   WISDOM
STRENGTH   GRACE/MERCY
BEAUTY
SPLENDOR   VICTORY
FOUNDATION
(God's action in the world)
KINGDOM
(the gate of prayer and spirituality)

A modern restatement of the Tree of Life stresses how the divine qualities or energies can flow to the world through men and women who become channels of divine creative life force. The divine attributes become human potentialities:

the Creator
power of Love   power of Wisdom
power of Intention   power of Compassion
power of Creativity
power of Observation   power of the Eternal Now
power of Manifesting
power of Healing

In appropriating these divine qualities, followers of Kabbalah depict each of them corresponding to a part of the human body: the first three (the crown—the mystery of the Infinite—in addition to wisdom and understanding) are represented, appropriately, by the head; strength by the left arm, and mercy by the right; the torso symbolizes beauty while splendor and victory are represented by the legs. The foundation (God's action in the world) is represented by the life-giving loins, while the person appropriating these qualities stands on the feet of the kingdom (the gate of prayer and spirituality). The Tree of Life and the Body are kinds of charts that enable one to appreciate an overview of God's powers as they energize human life, and they convey a sense of interrelationship between the qualities and a call to wholeness and harmony.

Let's see now what Cordovero tells us:

> Those who are proficient in kabbalah are able to consciously channel G-d's blessing and beneficence into the world. This is achieved through the process of *kavanah*, "intention," (pl. *kavanot*)—kabbalistically formulated meditations used during prayer or while fulfilling a *mitzvah* (commandment). It is through *kavanah* that the *sefirot* become properly harmonized and united, allowing the divine efflux to flow down, and the soul of the person practicing the *kavanah* (called a *mechaven*) becomes a channel through which G-d pours out His benevolence.
>
> He becomes the abode of the *Shechinah*.
>
> When the *mechaven* cleaves (*devekut*) to his Creator in thought and in deed (by fulfilling the *mitzvot*) his soul rises up and is elevated from level to level, from principle to principle and from cause to cause, until He pours out upon him a great outflow of beneficence so

that eventually this righteous person can become the seat and locus of outflow for the entire world. He becomes the abode of the *Shechinah* and the node through which G-d's blessing issues forth to the world. The *mechaven* therefore bears great responsibility towards his fellow man; at the same time, he is a greatly privileged individual.

When meditating, the *mechaven* does not focus on the *sefirot* per se, but rather on the *atzmut* (the Infinite Light) illuminating the *sefirot*—his prayer is "to Him, not to His attributes." Proper *kavanah* focuses upon G-d as He is when acting through the *sefira* hof *mercy* for example, or through *strength*. The Essential Name of G-d represented by the four-letter Tetragrammaton—*Yud-Hei-Vav-Hei*, is indicative of the Infinite Light clothed within the *sefirot*. Each *sefira* is distinguished from the others by the manner in which the Infinite Light is clothed within it . . .

One who is versed in kabbalah knows how to act at the right time by knowing which *sefirah* dominates at a particular time, and he cleaves to the light of the dominant *sefirah*. He can then bring about the correct adjustment and harmonization of the *sefirot* through proper thought, speech and deed. In this way a person extricates himself from lack of awareness of G-d, which may be compared to sleep and death, and binds himself to holiness and eternal life, which is the mystery of the *Garden of Eden*. Thus the Crown of the *Shechinah* never departs from his head.[6]

Clothes for the Great King

Kabbalah reaches a full flowering in the advent of the Hasidic movement, the mystical tradition founded by Israel Ben Eliezer (1700–1760), known as the Baal Shem Tov. He had the gift of bringing the mystical concepts of Kabbalah into people's everyday

6. Cordovero (trans. Miller), *Palm Tree,* chapter 10; Cordovero, "Soul Meditation" (https://www.chabad.org/Kabbalah/article_cdo/aid/380601/jewish/Soul-Meditation.ht/.).

lives. Heaven was brought down to earth![7] Let's listen to what he has to teach us:

> When you pray, visualize that G-d is invested within the letters of the prayers. You see, words are clothing for thoughts. As fine clothes bring out a person's inner beauty, so well-spoken words bring out your inner thoughts. They emerge from your personal world into the revealed world. So too, your words of prayer provide the same sort of clothing for G-d's presence.
>
> If so, you should be thinking, "This is a great king, and I am making clothes for Him! If so, I should do this with joy!"
>
> Put all your strength into those words, for this way you will attain oneness with Him. Since your energy is in your articulations of each letter, and in each letter G-d dwells, in this way you have become one with Him.[8]

Repairing the World

The sixteenth-century Kabbalist Isaac Luria (1534–1572) taught that in the mystery of creation, God poured his divine light into vessels over the world. These could not contain the effulgence of God's presence and shattered into many fragments, trapping sparks of the divine light amid their shards as they fell to earth. It is the vocation of humanity, taught Luria, to release and unlock these holy sparks amid the world's brokenness and return them to God through prayer and service. We are to discover the hidden presences of God amid the world's mire. We must discern opportunities for "gathering the sparks"—taking small steps to release the trapped glimmers of light that lie half buried in the dust of the world's confusions. Three things can inspire us about this vision of God's holiness. First, elements of divine light glint all around us, if only we open our eyes and look beneath the surface. Second, God asks us to work with him as partners in a divine-human synergy

7. See Scholem, *Major Trends*; and Green, ed., *Jewish Spirituality*.

8. From Baal Shem Tov, *Tzava'at Harivash* 108 (quoted in Freeman, "G-d in Your Words": https://www.chabad.org/).

of healing the fragmentedness of the world. Third, little actions, tiny steps of reconciliation matter very much and contribute to the restoration of wholeness bit by bit: do not despise the humble moments or small actions, because they help gather up a fragmented spark or two and return them to God. They help "repair the world."

Living out the Kabbalah

The Hasidic tradition aims to restore a sense of hopefulness, joy, and compassion into Jewish practice. A recent example illustrates this.

Ramleh was an Arab town, not so far from Jerusalem, until 1948, when Israeli forces removed the Arab population and repopulated the houses with newly arrived Jewish immigrants, fleeing the Europe that permitted the Holocaust and extermination camps. Dalia was a small child when her parents brought her to newly founded Israel in 1948 from Bulgaria. The family was assigned one of the former Arab homes, newly emptied: it had a lemon tree in the garden. Years passed, and one day in 1967 a teenage lad showed up at Dalia's house, with a couple of friends. Dalia, now a teenager herself, was on her own; her parents were out. The Arab lad explained that this was his father's house—his father had told him that it was the one with the lemon tree outside—and he just wanted to look around. Dalia welcomed him across the threshold. A friendship was formed.

After her parents died, and she inherited the house, Dalia opened it as a kindergarten where Jewish and Arab children could play together. She called it Open House.[9] Today Dalia leads interfaith sharings in Jerusalem, and I have been privileged to work alongside her in these. She says to me:[10]

> It is a challenge to stay with the pain of the mutual hurting between Palestinian Arab and Jew. You can either

9. The story is told in Tolan, *Lemon Tree.*

10. Dalia Landau (founder of Open House in Ramle), interview by Andrew Mayes, July 2011 at St George's College in Jerusalem.

run away from it, deny it, or maybe it is truer to live with the pain—that opens possibilities of healing. What we all need is an open heart, that enables us to hear the reality of the Other. The open heart opens the way to miracles: we are supernatural beings, not natural! When we really listen—not having our prepared answers—we can overcome the negative energy that comes from prejudice.

You can either picture Jerusalem—using biblical imagery—as bride or mother. A bride can have only one partner. But a mother can give nurture to many.

It all comes from the heart. We need to expand the heart, enlarge it: this can be a painful process and takes time. But Isaiah says [54:2]: "Enlarge the site of your tent." He was talking of the tent of your heart.[11]

Reflection: Questions

1. What strikes most you about this encounter of Kabbalah?

2. What does this chapter suggest about the relationship between prayer and life in the world—the inner life and the outer life?

3. How do you find yourself responding to the idea of the *sefirot*? What do they suggest about human dignity and vocation?

4. What situations invite you to practice *tikkun*? How would you go about it? What signs of repair would you be looking for?

Experience: Prayer Exercise

Either

Compose 18 blessings of your own based in the format

Blessed are You Lord King of the Universe, You . . . (add verb or divine action to celebrate God's providence in your life)

11. In the interfaith group I co-led with Dalia in Jerusalem, the main rule was "speak from the heart, not the head." It sought an experiential sharing not an analytical, academic discourse. See the Appendix for guidelines used.

OR

Meditate on the 10 divine *sefirot* or divine qualities. Slowly make your way down the Tree of Life, beginning at the top. Take time to savor and enjoy each of the qualities, praying that their energy may flow into you. You can light ten tealights, in turn, helping you realize that these *sefirot* are aspects of the divine light. Or you can pray that these qualities become embodied in you by visualizing that they abide in the respective parts of your body using the outline above. Conclude by praying a blessing on the world around you, that these divine energies may help to heal the brokenness of our world.

Further Reading

Bokser, Ben Zion. *The Jewish Mystical Tradition.* Northvale, NJ: Aronson, 1993.

Dan, Joseph, and Frank Talmage, eds. *Studies in Jewish Mysticism.* Cambridge, MA: Association for Jewish Studies, 1982.

Freeman, Rabbi Tzvi. *Bringing Heaven Down to Earth: 365 Meditations from the Wisdom of the Rebbe.* Vancouver, BC: Class One, 2002.

Jacobs, Louis, ed. *Jewish Mystical Testimonies.* New York: Schocken, 1977.

Scholem, Gershom. *Major Trends in Jewish Mysticism.* London: Thames & Hudson, 1955.

FIGURE 3

3

Through Zion Gate

Entering Armenian and Syriac Prayer

Invitation

ZION GATE IS so called because this part of the city had been
identified by the first Christians as "Holy Zion" where the sites of
the Last Supper and Pentecost are located. In Arabic it is called
Bab an-Nabi Dawud—Prophet David Gate—because David's
tomb is nearby. Pilgrims arriving today at Zion Gate are shocked
to see how badly it is pockmarked and honeycombed by holes
made by Jordanian bullets in 1948 or by Israeli snipers in 1967.
This wounded gate leads to two historic but fragile and vulnerable communities. As we step through its portals we can turn left
to discover the world of Armenian Orthodox spirituality. As we
turn right and take the historic Habad Street, the ancient Cardo
Maximus (north/south street), we stumble on the hidden treasures
of Syriac Orthodox spirituality.

Encounter

Meeting Armenians

Christians from Armenia—the first nation to embrace Christianity—came to Jerusalem in the fourth century as pilgrims and refugees. Armenian monk Fr. Emmanuel, wearing his distinctive black robes and pointed headgear, which evokes beloved Mount Ararat, welcomes me into the glittering interior of Saint James Armenian Orthodox Cathedral. It shimmers with what looks like a thousand oil lamps of different colors suspended from the ceiling, while rich carpets cover the floor. The altar is mounted on a stage called the *bema*, and a curtain is drawn across this at solemn moments of the liturgy.[1]

> The liturgy is the central part of our prayer. Jesus gave us the Eucharist at the Last Supper when he took bread and wine and declared it to be his body and blood. In our iconography we see angels holding a chalice in their hands at the crucifixion, receiving the blood of Christ. When I see this it reminds me that Christians should expect martyrdom and persecution. Certainly, that has been the experience of Armenians through the ages, from the times they first came here as refugees to the genocide of the last century. Indeed we have here the relics of Saint James, the brother of the Lord, first bishop of Jerusalem, who died a martyr's death. We need to withstand the devil's attacks—that's why we pray "deliver us from evil." The Eucharist always reminds me of sacrifice.
>
> But it's about regaining paradise too and anticipating heaven. Look and see the stars in the arch—that speaks to us of heaven. And see how in Armenian art the cross is a tree of life—at the corners of the cross there are buds of new life—the cross is the tree of life, which leads us back to paradise.
>
> But we also pray as monks in our cells alone. Jesus said, "Go to your secret place and shut the door." There we contemplate, we pray from the heart. We go step by step

1. Fr. Emmanuel, monk of Armenian monastery, interview by Andrew Mayes, March 2018 at St James Convent in Jerusalem.

up to God. We confess our sins and declare our love to God. Step by step we gain experience and move towards the kingdom of heaven. When we contemplate we think of the mysteries of our faith, especially the incarnation and the sacrament. We contemplate the Word of God. We grow in our relationship with God the Holy Trinity, who reveals himself to us as Father, Son, and Holy Spirit. We follow the steps of the saints, who train us through their teaching—especially the *Lives of the Holy Fathers* and the *Sayings of the Desert Fathers*, a collection we call "the Paradise." We read it every day.

So you see we try to balance our prayer. Sometimes we are together as a community at the Holy Altar. Other times we are in solitude in our cell, alone with God. We need both!

Kevork Hintlian has served as Secretary to the Armenian patriarch over many years. A distinguished historian, he brings a longer perspective to the current situation.[2]

It is a continual struggle these days, so many years un-der occupation. We have been here for fifteen centuries and now we are struggling to keep the continuity of witness unbroken. Today, the Armenian community in Jerusalem numbers only about 1,200. It stood at two thousand about ten years ago. But the School (primary and secondary) continues to hold out hope for the future as new generations of Armenians are trained. The Semi-nary, training new deacons and priests, has fifty students aged fifteen to twenty-three. Until 1990 they were drawn largely from Syria and Lebanon; this is no longer pos-sible, and today they come from Armenia itself. While this strengthens the cultural ethos of the Seminary, the students today can't speak Arabic like their predecessors, so engagement with the local community is very limited. They feel isolated and cut off.

Like the Holy Fire each Easter in the Church of the Resurrection, we must rekindle the flame continu-ally, we must ensure a continuity of light. You know, the

2. Kevork Hintlian (historian), interview by Andrew Mayes in November 2010 at Swedish Centre on Armenian Patriarchate Road.

Holy Fire ceremony in the Church of the Resurrection is very symbolic to us. It has taken place every Easter for hundreds of years. Before the ceremony, they affix a huge wax seal over the door of the tomb of Christ. Then the Armenian patriarch and the Greek patriarch disrobe in humility and break the seal and enter the tomb. The whole church is in a heightened state of expectancy. After five minutes—it feels like an eternity—they emerge with the holy fire of the resurrection. When people pass it around they put the flame on their faces as if taking in some mysterious power. We Armenians say, "You are my brother, you are my sister" when the flame is passed from person to person. It gives us hope and identity. The Greeks say it is a miracle that is repeated each Easter. For me, the miracle is the continuity. We must not let the flame go out. Even when it is difficult: you know that Christians on the West Bank, only a few miles away, are not allowed to attend the Easter ceremony. So they wait for the fire to reach them: by taxi, by car, by motorbike, it is taken all over the Occupied Territories, crossing barriers and checkpoints. That is the miracle. The fire is unquenchable and it must spread.

For the Armenian community right now it is more a question of survival than resurrection or renaissance. It is easy to become demoralized, and lose faith in humanity. But we do not lose faith in God. We must believe that he will protect his flock. The resurrection sustains us and keeps hope alive.

Meeting Syriacs

A labyrinth of narrow streets leads us ultimately to the Syriac Orthodox Church of Saint Mark, a gem tucked away in the heart of the city. The church is ancient and preserves the memory of the Last Supper. Fr. Shem'on, the senior monk here, came to the Holy Land forty years ago, after monastic training at the fourth-century monastery of Deir Al Zafaran on Tur Abdin—the Mountain of the Servants of God—in southeast Turkey, where he was born. Wearing the characteristic Syriac clergy's black headscarf with thirteen white crosses (representing the apostles and Christ), and wiping a tear from his eye, Fr. Shem'on explains:[3]

> Today the Syriac community feels vulnerable and marginalized. We are an ancient church, but a fragile community today—we just have one hundred families left in the Old City, and we grieve for our people in Syria.
>
> But let us rejoice in the cross and resurrection. Jesus is the Second Adam. The first Adam lost wisdom and faith when he grasped the fruit from the tree of knowledge. But Jesus dies here at Calvary on another tree. He leads us back to paradise. He ends our exile from God. The wood of the cross brings us salvation. The resurrection means the renewal of our lives each day. We can live with strong faith and love, if we look straight at the Risen One and his commandments. What we have to do each day is to exercise ourselves, discipline ourselves to make sure that our actions, our character, and our nature are as he wants. Each one has to recover himself and direct himself to the teaching of the Lord.
>
> The resurrection isn't just an event of long ago! The resurrection means new life for the world, a new beginning. It is an eternal victory over death, Satan, and sin that we must claim each day. We live the resurrection each day, every day. It does not belong to the past long ago. It is for today. The resurrection gives a new life daily for a person who looks to heaven. Don't always think of earth, of materialism, which causes heaviness. In the Gospel of Matthew Jesus says: "Come to me all you who are heavy laden and I will give you rest. Take my yoke and learn from me, for I am humble of heart . . ." That is how we should live in the Holy City. We should give our burdens to the Lord. We must live humbly. We must keep learning from Jesus. And he gives us rest, true security in this world of turmoil. But we need to find solitude and silence to truly feel the rest in our soul. We need to stand still before the Living God and think it through. And that renews us, heart, mind, and body for life in this world.

3. Fr. Shem'on, monk of Syrian monastery, interview by Andrew Mayes in March 2011 at St Mark's Convent in Jerusalem.

Sister Jostina in Jerusalem is a lay sister and guide at Saint Mark's Syriac Church. In her fifties, with a big, round face, wearing a black headscarf, she moves her arms in the air excitedly as she speaks.[4]

> Welcome to this holy place—the upper room of the house down. (People ask me why the Upper Room is downstairs. If you want anything old in Jerusalem you always have to go down!) This is a place of many miracles. I have witnessed five miracles of healing in front of this icon of the Virgin Mary painted by Saint Luke on skin of deer. What is important to us in this place is receiving the Holy Spirit, because the first Pentecost happened right here! We experience what happened at the very beginning of Christianity, in the book of Acts chapter 2. The apostles spoke and people from different nations asked "how is it that we hear, each of us in his own language?" Last year a Russian Israeli visitor arrived: he asked me questions in Hebrew, but I received them in English. I speak only English and of course Aramaic, the language of Jesus, the tongue of our community here. I answered him in English, but he received my words in Hebrew. Praise be to God! In this place we seek to receive the Holy Spirit often. I am the church cleaner, and I pray, "Lord as I clean the church, please clean my heart!" So I will be ready to receive the Holy Spirit again!

Discovery

Treasures from Armenian Spirituality

Armenian prayer is a paschal spirituality, deeply marked by the cross and resurrection, which has been experienced in the nation's life through the centuries, not least through the massacres of 1915, the Armenian genocide. In their own lives, Armenians identify with both the pain and suffering of crucifixion, and with hopefulness and resurgence springing from resurrection and new

4. Sr. Jostina (lay sister of Syrian monastery), interview by Andrew Mayes in January 2010 at St Mark's Convent in Jerusalem.

beginnings. Two classic writers lead us right into the heart of Armenian spirituality.

The tenth-century author Gregory of Narek (945–1003) is hailed as the best representative of medieval Armenian spirituality—indeed as one of the greatest Christian mystics of all time. He is little discovered outside the Armenian church—though he is beginning to be enjoyed since Pope Francis declared him to be a Doctor of the Church in 2015. Gregory became abbot of the monastery on the shores of Lake Van in historic Armenia. Considered the first poet of the Armenians, Gregory gathered together ninety-five stunning prayers in a work called *Speaking with God from the Depths of the Heart*, which he called an "encyclopedia of prayer for all nations," hoping it might be a guide to prayer for people around the world. Now we can enjoy this in the fresh translations that have been made.[5] It opens with these words:

> The voice of a sighing heart, its sobs and mournful cries,
> I offer up to you, O Seer of Secrets,
> placing the fruits of my wavering mind
> as a savory sacrifice on the fire of my grieving soul
> to be delivered to you in the censer of my will.

> Compassionate Lord, breathe in
> this offering and look more favorably on it
> than upon a more sumptuous sacrifice
> offered with rich smoke. Please find
> this simple string of words acceptable.
> Do not turn in disdain.

> May this unsolicited gift reach you,
> this sacrifice of words
> from the deep mystery-filled chamber

5. Also known as *Lamentations of Gregory of Narek*. See Gregory of Narek (trans. Samuelian), *Speaking with God*, prayer 1, p. 1. See also www.stgregoryofnarek.am.

of my feelings, consumed in flames
fueled by whatever grace I may have within me ...[6]
A new book of psalms sings with urgency through me,
for all thinking people the world over,
expressing all human passions
and serving with its images
as an encyclopedic companion to our human condition,
for the entire, mixed congregation of the
Church universal ...[7]

One of these prayers (Lamentation 33) has found its way into the Armenian liturgy and is said by the priest at the start of every Eucharist:

Almighty, beneficent God of all, who
loves mankind, maker of the visible and invisible,
savior and creator,
defender and peacemaker, spirit of the Father Almighty,
we beseech you with outstretched arms,
tears and prayers,
as we appear before you,
you, who strike terror in our hearts,
judge us as we approach with trembling and fear,
presenting first this sacrificial offering of
words to your power that is beyond understanding.
You share the throne, glory and creatorship of
the undiminishing honor of the Father.
You examine our deepest secrets and mysteries ...
Again, I shall continue in this manner
until the assurance of the miraculous light
heralds the good news of peace.
With all our souls

6. Gregory of Narek (trans. Samuelian), *Speaking with God*, prayer 1, page 1.

7. Gregory of Narek (trans. Samuelian), *Speaking with God*, prayer 3, p. 13.

we pray and beseech you with tearful cries,
glorious creator, incorruptible and uncreated,
timeless Holy Spirit of compassion.
You are the intercessor of our silent sighs to
your merciful Father.
You, who keep the saints, purify the sinners and
build the temple of the living and life-giving
will of the Father,
free me now from all unclean deeds,
which are not pleasing for your dwelling place.
Do not extinguish the light of grace
in us and in our minds' eye,
for we have learned that you will join us
through prayer . . .[8]

Nersēs Shnorhali (1102–1173)—his name means "grace-filled"—was an outstanding theologian, poet, composer, and historian. As leader of the Armenian church (*Catholicos*) he was deeply involved in attempts at ecumenical reconciliation with the Greek and Latin churches. His hymns are deeply loved, and his hymn *I confess with faith* is sung every Lent:

I confess with faith and worship you,
Father, Son and Holy Spirit,
uncreated and immortal Essence,
creator of angels, humans and of all that exists.
Have mercy upon your creatures,
and on me, a manifold sinner . . .

I confess with faith and worship you,
O Indivisible Light,
unified Holy Trinity and one Godhead;
creator of light and dispeller of darkness,

8. Gregory of Narek (trans. Samuelian), *Speaking with God*, 151.

dispel from my soul the darkness of sin and ignorance,
and enlighten my mind at this moment,
so that I may pray to you according to your will,
and receive from you the fulfillment of my requests.
Have mercy upon your creatures,
and on me, a manifold sinner . . .[9]

O Christ, the quickening fire,
inflame my soul with the fire of your love
that you dispersed over the earth,
so that it may consume the stains of my soul;
cleanse my conscience and my mind,
purify my body from sin,
and kindle the light of your knowledge in my heart . . .[10]

In his long poem *Jesus, Son, Only-Begotten of the Father*, Nersēs takes a personal reading of the parables and episodes of the Old Testament and the Gospels, locating himself as participant and recipient in the action, identifying himself with the characters. For him, it is experience and involvement and engagement with the sacred text that matters. For example, here is his reading of the parable of the Good Samaritan, and his journey from Jerusalem to Jericho:

From Salem, which is Paradise
For us and Adam, first to sin,
It was I who went to Jericho
And fell into the hands of thieves.

They robbed me of Thy Light, and filled
My soul with painful wounds . . .

9. https://shnorhali.com/english/
10. Nersēs, Shnorhali, *I Confess with Faith*.

Anoint the depths of my poor soul,
And clothe me with the former robe
Of which the robbers stripped me bare.
Put oil and wine—the salve of life—
Upon my wounded soul.

Anoint anew my heart. Give me
The Cup of Thy New Covenant
To drink: raise me upon Thy Cross
And take me to the Inn—Thy Church.[11]

The twelfth-century Armenian poet reads the story of John 4 with longing:

O Fountain of life, you asked for water from the woman of Samaria,
And promised her living water,
in return for the transitory one.
Grant to me, O Fountain of Life,
That holy drink for my soul,
That flows from the heart in rivers,
The Spirit from whom grace gushes forth.[12]

Recalling the Last Supper, Nersēs desires that he is right there among the disciples:

Thou who made known the mysteries
Of Thy redeeming Cross, one eve,
Giving Thy Body and Thy Blood
That Thy Disciples might have life,
Admit me to their holy ranks:
Let me partake of Food Divine,
The Bread of Life for which I yearn,
And of Thy Cup for which I thirst . . .[13]

---

11. Nersēs, *Jesus, Son, Only Begotten of the Father*, 94.
12. Nersēs Schnorhali, *Jesus, the Son*, 45.
13. Nersēs Schnorhali, *Jesus, the Son*, 121.

Treasures from Syriac Spirituality

Ephrem, the Syrian poet, hymn-writer, and deacon of the fourth century (d. 373), tells us to approach the search with a loving desire:

> Whenever I have meditated upon You
> I have acquired a veritable treasure from You . . .
> Your treasury seems empty to the person who rejects You.
> Love is the treasurer
> Of Your heavenly treasure store . . .[14]

Within the rich heritage of the Syriac spiritual tradition, Saint Ephrem represents an outstanding example. His great *Hymn on Faith* uses powerful imagery and metaphors to describe the spiritual life:

> See, Fire and Spirit are in the womb of her who bore You;
> See, Fire and Spirit are in the river in which You were baptized.
> Fire and Spirit are in our baptismal font,
> In the Bread and the Cup are Fire and Holy Spirit[15]

In this poem Ephrem celebrates the mysterious working of the Holy Spirit in the Eucharist and in the spiritual life. Echoing the story of the Syrophoenician woman (Mark 7) he writes,[16]

> Look, Lord, my lap is now filled with the crumbs from Your table
> there is no more room in the folds of my garment,
> So hold back Your gift as I worship before You,
> Keep it in Your treasure house in readiness
> to give it us on another occasion.

There certainly are many "other occasions"—for Ephrem was a prolific and inspiring writer. He encourages us to see reality

---

14. Brock, trans., *Luminous Eye,* 44.

15. Brock, trans., *Luminous Eye,* 108.

16. Brock, trans., *Luminous Eye,* 40.

differently, using his famed image of the "luminous eye," which can look into the hiddenness of God's mystery:

> Blessed is the person who has acquired a luminous eye
> With which he will see how much the angels stand in awe of
> You, Lord,
> And how audacious is man.[17]

Ephrem encourages us to pray for the gift of the inner eye, which penetrates the deep things of God and gives true in-sight. In this way our prayer can become luminous, radiant, and light-revealing, as he says in his *Hymn on the Church*:

> Let our prayer be a mirror, Lord, placed before Your face;
> Then Your fair beauty will be imprinted on its luminous surface
> . . .[18]

One of Saint Ephrem's prayers is said twice daily by Syriacs in Lent, accompanied by prostrations. A prostration, made after each part of the prayer, is a full bow to the ground with the knees touching the ground, and the head touching or near the ground. After each prostration, the supplicant immediately stands up again. As the bow to the ground is begun, the sign of the cross is made. Some people touch their knees to the ground first and then bend their upper body down, while others fall forward to the ground, knees and hands touching at the same time. "O God, cleanse me, a sinner" is said twelve times, with a bow each time. At each bow the sign of the cross is made, the head bowed by bending at the waist: some bow deeply and touch the ground with their right hand.[19]

> O Lord and Master of my life, give me not a spirit of idleness,
> despondency, ambition, or vain talking.
> But rather a spirit of purity, humility, patience and love, bestow
> upon me Thy servant. (prostration)

17. Brock, trans., *Luminous Eye*, 73.

18. Brock, trans., *Luminous Eye*, 75.

19. This explanation and translation of the prayer is taken from www.orthodox.net/.

Yea, O Lord and King, grant me to see my own faults and not
to judge my brother, for blessed art Thou unto the ages of ages.
Amen. (prostration)
O God, cleanse me, a sinner. (twelve times, with a bow made
for each)[20]

Isaac the Syrian (613–700) tells how God seizes the soul and
leads the person into a state of divine madness so that the person
becomes a fool for Christ, becomes inebriated with God. In the
Syriac, the term "inebriation" is linked linguistically to the term
"wonder" or "amazement":

> Sometimes, while prayer remains for its part, the intel-
> lect is taken away from it as if into heaven, and tears fall
> like fountains of waters, involuntarily soaking the whole
> face. All this time such a person is serene, still and filled
> with a wonder-filled vision . . . he remains continually in
> amazement at God's work in creation—like people who
> are crazed by wine, for this is the "wine which causes
> the person's heart to rejoice" (Ps 104:15). Blessed is the
> person who has entered this door in the experience of his
> own soul, for all the power of ink, letters and phrases is
> too feeble to indicate the delight of this mystery.[21]

Isaac represents well the Syriac tradition in his beautiful
prayer, which we can make our own:

> O mystery exalted beyond every word and beyond si-
> lence, who became human in order to renew us by means
> of your voluntary union with the flesh, reveal to me the
> path by which I may be raised up to your mysteries,
> traveling along a course that is clear and tranquil, free
> from the illusions of this world. Gather my mind into
> the silence of prayer, so that wandering thoughts may
> be silenced within me during that luminous converse of
> supplication and mystery-filled wonder.[22]

20. Holy Trinity Monastery, *Prayer Book*, 152.

21. Alfeyev, *Spiritual World*, 249.

22. Quoted in Isaac, Bishop of Nineveh, *Prayers of Saint Isaac*, Prayer 7.

Reflection: Questions

1. What strikes you most from the interviews with Armenians and Syriacs?

2. What approaches in the spirituality of the Armenians resonate with your experience?

3. What aspects of the ancient Syriac writers hearten or challenge you?

4. How do you find yourself responding to Father Emmanuel's words: "When I see a chalice, it reminds me that Christians should expect martyrdom and persecution"?

5. How do you respond to Father Shem'on's affirmation: "We live the resurrection each day, every day"?

Experience: Prayer Exercise

Following the example of Nersēs Shnorhali, take an episode or a parable from the Gospels and read yourself there (a pattern of prayer that Ignatius of Loyola was to develop).

Further Reading

Brock, Sebastian. *The Syriac Fathers on Prayer and the Spiritual Life.* Cistercian Studies Series 101. Kalamazoo, MI: Cistercian, 1987.

Hintlian, Kevork. *History of the Armenians in the Holy Land.* Jerusalem: St. James, 1976.

Ormanian, Malachia. *The Church of Armenia: Her History, Doctrine, Rule, Discipline, Liturgy, Literature, and Existing Condition.* Translated by G. Marcar Gregory. 1912. Reprint, London: Forgotten Books, 2018.

Prior, Michael, and William Taylor, eds. *Christians in the Holy Land.* London: World of Islam Festival Trust, 1994.

FIGURE 4

4

Through the New Gate

Encountering Franciscan and Orthodox Spiritualities

Invitation

THE ARCHED GATE, DECORATED with crenelated stonework, was opened in the northern wall of the city only in 1889, to enable access to the Christian holy places from the new estates developing outside the city walls. It leads the pilgrim to the most sacred site of the Holy Sepulcher, or as locals call it, the Church of the Resurrection, the basilica which encompasses both the scarred and sacred rock of Calvary and the empty tomb of Christ. The New Gate thus summons us to newness of life as the pilgrim encounters the cross and the resurrection. Here East meets West as the church is shared by six different Christian communities, principally the Franciscan and Greek Orthodox. So this chapter is in two parts. First we encounter the *Franciscan tradition,* and enter into its spirituality, springing from Francis's experience of the cross and the resurrection, discovering for ourselves the practice of the "cross prayers." Second, we meet with the Greek patriarch and bishop of Jerusalem, and are invited to encounter the *Orthodox spirituality* of the divine light.

Encounter: The Franciscans

Alleyways lead us down, through the labyrinthine Christian Quarter, to the astounding Church of the Holy Sepulcher. A Franciscan chapel marks the place beside the crest of Calvary's rock where the soldiers pinned Jesus to the wood of the cross. Ten Franciscan brothers live in the friary adjacent to the basilica, coming from seven different countries—Ireland, Ghana, the Philippines, Poland, the United States, Brazil, and Korea. Italian is the lingua franca for this an international community and Father Fergus, an Irish priest, is its superior.[1]

> This is the Church in microcosm! We have the continual challenge of expressing ourselves clearly across the cultures, trying to understand each other and sometimes not! As we develop our spirituality in this place, we have a saying: "There is no night here!" This is true in two senses, at least. First, we pray through the night. We hardly go to bed—we have perhaps only four and a half hours of sleep! This is the rhythm of our prayer: in the early evening we have Vespers, Compline, and the Procession. At a quarter to midnight we gather to say the Night Office, the Office of Readings, and Morning Prayer, 'til 12:30. At 4.30 a.m. we have a mass at the Tomb. At ten past six we say the office of Terce [morning prayer]and have our community Eucharist. We will also have five masses before dawn at different altars in the Church because this is required by the Status Quo [the order of services established under Ottoman times]. But of course, there is no night here is a second sense: Christ has abolished the night of sin and death!
>
> It is the greatest privilege to live by Calvary and the Empty Tomb. I say to the pilgrims: forget the archaeology for a moment. The thing is: the greatest event in the history of humanity happened HERE! I live the Resurrection by speaking it, proclaiming it to the pilgrims. The more I share it, the deeper it gets. I tell them at the

---

1. Fr. Fergus Clarke (then superior of the Franciscan Monastery), interview by Andrew Mayes in November 2010 at the Franciscan Monastery, Church of the Holy Sepulcher.

anointing stone: "Leave your tears here. Leave your fail-ures, your frustrations, your fears here. Leave your hopes here. Leave this place free—free to proclaim that Jesus Christ is alive!" Our role here is to proclaim the gospel and offer hospitality to pilgrims.

Saint Jerome, when he was living beside the birth-place of Jesus in Bethlehem, said something like, "It's not a big deal to live here. The big deal is to live the gospel!" This place can be chaotic with the number of visitors, and I have to continually talk to myself about the res-urrection, and about seeing the Risen Christ in others, like he says in Matthew 25—to see Jesus in the poor and the broken. I have to stay mindful of these things. When things get stressful here—like thousands arriving from the cruise ships just as we start our procession, I have to keep calm. I think of Paul saying, "God chooses the weak . . ." First Corinthians 1 is one of my favorite passages. It tells me that it is God's work not mine: his treasure in earthen vessels. This is how I cope with the hordes of people. I say to myself: "Stay calm. Live the resurrection! Show hospitality!"

I am continually inspired by the example of Saint Francis. Remember, Francis sent the friars here. He was fascinated by the humanity of God—the idea that God chose to become human. Every breath we take speaks of the reality of the incarnation. God didn't come for just two weeks—he come to share our life so completely—he perspired, the thirsted, he fatigued—it was real. That is why we are here—the unfolding of God's embrace of humanity happened here. Francis wanted his brothers to live at the places of salvation.

But more than this, he modeled reconciliation, es-pecially in his visit to the Muslim sultan at Damietta in 1219. In a sense we see Francis's failure as a missionary here, but in another sense, it was a powerful witness, and a relationship of real respect developed between Francis and the sultan. So we Franciscans try to reflect the at-titude of Francis in this. We get pilgrims in here and we get unbelievers. Our presence here sometimes provokes questions: "Who are these brown-robed Franciscans? What do they stand for?" This is our ministry. I think of

the parable of the sower. Our task is to scatter the seeds.
Some visitors will be open, some not. Some pilgrims
want a holiday with five-star hotels and a swimming
pool. Others come to seek the Risen Christ. It is a joy
to see pilgrims visibly moved in this place, to hear their
singing and their prayers. I hope that they will go out
from here more able to proclaim the gospel in a clear and
effective way! Christ is Risen!

Discovery: Franciscan Spirituality of the Cross

Most High,

glorious God,

enlighten the darkness of my heart

and give me

true faith,

certain hope,

and perfect charity,

sense and knowledge,

Lord,

that I may carry out

Your holy and true command.[2]

This prayer that Francis uttered, kneeling before the figure of the
Crucified above the altar in the ruined chapel of San Damiano in
Assisi in 1207, celebrates an encounter with the cross that proves
to be a profound moment in his conversion and the radical re-
orientation of his life towards God. Looking at the cross he heard
the words, "Francis, rebuild my church, which as you can see is
falling down." His prayer is about vocation; about self-offering;
about discovering God's will; about being empowered by love,
hope, and faith. It is a prayer that will change his life and lead him
to rebuild the church on true gospel values. Carlo Carretto puts
Francis' response like this:

2. Armstrong et al., eds., *Francis of Assisi*, 1:40.

I must confess that in that moment I was thunderstruck at the mystery of Christ's incarnation . . .the idea of God's incarnation that became the only answer to all the self-questionings hitherto in my life. Jesus was the epitome of all: in him heaven and earth resolved all their contradictions in one stupendous, vital act of divine unity, satisfying every human thirst. Jesus' Cross was humanity's happiness, love's answer to all the questions, the resolution of every conflict, the overcoming of every tension, God's victory over death.[3]

What was it about the cross that so transfixed Francis? He glimpsed that God himself comes to share and transfigure our pain. God is not immune from suffering—he freely chooses to embrace it, and to transform it from the *inside*—not from the outside as some external power reaching down from the balcony of heaven, but *as one of us*. "Surely he has borne our griefs and carried our sorrows" (Isa 53:4). In his *Testament* Francis put it this way: "It was the Father's will that his blessed and glorious Son, whom he gave to us and who was born for our sake, should offer himself . . . leaving us an example that we may follow in his steps (1 Pet 2:21) . . . how peaceful, delightful, loveable and desirable above all things it is to have a Brother like this!"[4]

Francis began to recognize the cross in daily life by a chance encounter with a leper on the road outside Assisi. Normally, he recoiled at the sight of these disfigured and disabled sufferers. In fact, he had an absolute horror of them and would avoid going near their colonies at all costs. But something stirred within his heart when he met this tortured man in the lane, with bandaged hands and dressed in rags. He felt impelled, constrained by something within, not only to approach the man, but to touch him tenderly, to embrace him. Later he wondered if he had not met Christ himself in this encounter.[5]

3. Carretto, *I, Francis*, 33.

4. Quoted in Habig, ed., *St. Francis of Assisi*, 93, 96.

5. Poignantly, in his own words, Francis describes this as a turning point in his life: "This is how God inspired me, Brother Francis, to embark upon a life of penance. When I was in sin, the sight of lepers nauseated me beyond

Francis saw a connection between present human suffering and the cross of Jesus Christ on Calvary. He saw God sharing and *redeeming*—literally "buying back" or "taking ownership of"—our pains. Revulsion at suffering turned to compassion in the literal meaning of that word—as Francis learned to *suffer with* those who were hurting. Francis too woke up to the idea that God is speaking to us in suffering, calling us to face up to the most important things in life. C. S. Lewis put it powerfully: "God whispers to us in our pleasures, speaks to us in our conscience, but shouts to us in our pains: it is his megaphone to rouse a deaf world."[6] Lewis suggests that the experience of pain can shatter the illusion that all is well with us, destroying the false idea that we can get very nicely by without God. Pain shatters the illusion of self-sufficiency, for it causes us to reach out to God. It wakes us up to the big questions of God and evil, and can draw us into a new surrender to God, the communion for which we were created. As we encounter the cross in our prayers, it confronts us with the problem of evil, and connects us with those who suffer violence, terrorism, or attack today.

Francis came to see in every suffering person a glimpse of the crucified Christ. Francis believed that suffering does indeed have a revelatory character, for those with eyes to see it. For Francis God speaks most powerfully through the experience of poverty and pain, calling us to simplicity and trust. For him, though he delighted in the wonders of creation, God's love was revealed most clearly in the passion of Jesus. He came to see the cross, an instrument of torture, as a symbol of hope: "by his wounds, you are healed" (1 Pet 2:22). From this self-same cross flows a grace which can change our attitudes to pain profoundly.

Francis's whole life was marked by the experience of suffering, hardship, and debilitating illness. He looked on these experiences as a way of uniting himself with Jesus Christ, whom he

---

measure; but then God himself led me into their company, and I had pity on them. When I had once become acquainted with them, what had previously nauseated me became a source of spiritual and physical consolation for me . . . we bless you, because by your holy Cross you have redeemed the world" (Habig, *St Francis*, 67).

6. Lewis, *Problem of Pain*, 81, 83.

understood as God's love and compassion incarnate. He accepted that his vocation was to walk in the steps of the Crucified One, and to reveal to others the power of the cross. Brother Thomas of Celano, Francis's first biographer, describes how he was graced to see pain in this light: "Since Francis was thus worn out in every part by sufferings, it is surprising that his strength was sufficient to bear them. But he looked upon these trials not under the name of sufferings but of *sisters*."[7]

It was in solitude on Mount Verna, praying for the grace to feel in his heart the intense love enkindled in Christ, that Francis received the gift of the stigmata, receiving in his feet and hands, and in his side, an impression of the five wounds of the crucified Christ. This was the culmination of a life dedicated to penetrating the mystery of the cross. For him the words came literally true: "I have been crucified with Christ; it is no longer I who live, but Christ who lives in me; and the life I now live in the flesh I live by faith in the Son of God, who loved me and gave himself for me" (Gal 3:20). Carretto puts it this way: "When I realized that I had holes in my hands and feet, and especially that I had a wound in my side, I understood what it meant to live without trifling. Love is indeed a serious thing, a terrible challenge."[8] Francis realized in that moment that through the cross the Christian is invited to be fired, energized, empowered, transfigured, healed by such love.

Encounter: The Orthodox

The New Gate ushers us towards the palatial residence of the Greek Orthodox bishop of Jerusalem. His Beatitude Theophilos III tells me:[9]

> The patriarchate is a sign of the Risen Christ in the Old City. Our churches are full. We live out our prayers and

7. Quoted in Habig, ed., *St. Francis of Assisi,* 532.

8. Caretto, *I, Francis,* 130.

9. His Beatitude Patriarch Theophilos III (patriarch of the Holy City of Jerusalem and all Palestine and Israel), interview by Andrew Mayes in November 2010 at the Greek Orthodox Patriarchate in Jerusalem.

proclaim his life in our School of St Demetrius, our Good Samaritan Centre for the Elderly, the Arab Ortho-dox Society for the Relief of the Sick, and its St Bene-dictos Medical Center. There is the social club and the scouts with their band. But it is so difficult to get people to stay in the Old City, and Christians are emigrating all the time—our presence is diminishing steadily. Families cannot afford the school fees and the rents. The poor are becoming poorer and the rich are becoming richer, and there is a bigger separation between them. But the pil-grims remind us that we are not alone. They encourage us.

I saw a mother by our door the other day, with her little boy. He was looking up and admiring our beauti-ful doors. Beauty lifts up the heart. But the greatest beauty of the Risen Christ is in our worship. The liturgy makes the mystery of the resurrection come alive for us. People experience the risen Christ in the worship of the Church—the Divine Liturgy. You reveal what is happen-ing on the inside by what comes out. You can tell what is in people's hearts by looking at their faces in worship. In the worship at the Holy Places, they are alive, radi-ant. You see wonder and joy on their faces, dignity, glory. You see, what goes on the mind—the Logos—the Word of God, this is an inner reality and thought, but it comes out in so many ways. It comes out in the spoken greeting "*Christos Aneste*! Christ is risen!" But it comes out most in our lives, living with courage and hope in the heart of the City.

His Beatitude opens the resource *Jerusalem: Navel of the World*, showing me dramatic pictures of the Holy Fire ceremony in the Basilica of the Resurrection and talks about this symbol of hope which sustains and heartens the Christians of Jerusalem. His photographs convey the excitement and anticipation of the Easter service, when thousands throng the church, standing on every available ledge, clinging to pillars, hanging from balconies. It seems that the whole world is here—there are Christians of every hue from every corner of the universal church. The focal point is the *edicule*, the house that covers and protects the cave-tomb of Christ.

The Orthodox patriarch, as the bishop of Jerusalem, breaks the seal on the tomb and prays in the deep darkness inside. The church is filled with both shadow and expectation. Awesomely, a new light is kindled in the darkness of the tomb. It is passed out of the tomb and spreads like wildfire among the pilgrims, each of whom has a bundle of thirty-three candles representing the earthly life of Christ. Their tapers become a radiant torch. The darkness is overcome and dispelled; the whole basilica is filled not only with light but with fire! Crashing church bells toll enthusiastically, and amid dancing and the great noise of ululations and exultant cheers, the fire is taken quickly outside to the waiting crowds. Runners then take it out of the city far and wide, to Christians on the occupied West Bank prevented from getting into Jerusalem each Easter, by plane to Orthodox in Greece . . .

His Beatitude reminds me that the Holy Fire flaming from the cave—representing the risen life of Christ among us—is a powerful symbol that the darkness cannot quench the light of Christ, that the light and hope of the Risen One is an inextinguishable blaze. As I look at the pictures with him, it strikes me that the divine fire of the resurrection is a risky and dangerous thing—health and safety police would have a fit! Hair is singed and clothes are scorched! But it is also, for the Christians of Jerusalem, highly contagious—passing from one to another—you can't keep it to yourself! The Christians here live their lives unselfconsciously and faithfully. The Holy Fire is a sign and promise of great comfort to the local Christians in the Holy Land. As one Jerusalemite Christian put it, "In a Good Friday world, we seek to live Easter."

Discovery: Orthodox Spirituality of Divine Light

Symeon the New Theologian (949–1022) was based in Constantinople where, for twenty-five years, he was abbot of Saint Mamas Monastery. He has been called in the east "the greatest mystic of the Middle Ages" and was surnamed "the New Theologian" by later admirers to identify him with such creative theologians as Saint John. He anticipated the later Byzantine *hesychast* movement with his teaching on personal communion with God in contemplation. His central conviction was that the Holy Spirit makes possible a conscious encounter with Christ and, in some sense, the vision of God in this life. In an age when doctrinal controversy divided the Greek and Latin churches—over the Western addition to the Nicene Creed ("We believe in the Holy Spirit, who proceeds from the Father *and the Son*")—Symeon taught that it is personal experience of the Spirit and God's kingdom which is paramount, within the eucharistic community of the church.

> But answer this question: What is the Holy Spirit? "God," you say, "we confess Him as true God from true God." Thus, as you see and in accordance with the dogmas of the Church, you say that He is God. So, too, by both saying and thinking that He is true God proceeding from true God, you establish that those who have the Holy Spirit have confessedly God dwelling always within themselves . . .
>
> Make no mistake! God is a fire, and has cast fire on the earth. The same Fire goes about looking for kindling to seize upon, for a ready disposition and will, in order to fall upon it and ignite it . . . when it has completely cleansed us of the filth of the passions, it becomes light and joy without ceasing in us, and by participation, it makes us light ourselves. It is like a clay pot that has been set on the fire. At first it is somewhat blackened by the smoke of the burning fuel, but after the fuel has begun to burn fiercely, then it becomes all translucent and like the fire itself, and the smoke can communicate none of its blackness to it. Just so, indeed, does the soul which has begun to burn with divine longing see first of all the murk of its passions within it, billowing out like smoke in the fire of the Holy Spirit . . . After these things have been utterly destroyed . . . then the divine and immaterial fire unites itself essentially to the soul, too, and the latter is immediately kindled and becomes transparent, and shares in it like the clay pot does in the visible fire . . .
>
> What else is so dear to God and welcome as a contrite and humble heart, and pride laid low in a spirit of humility? It is in such a condition of soul that God Himself comes to dwell and make His rest.

Have mercy on me, Son of David, and open the eyes
of my soul, so that I may see the light of the world, even
You, Who are God, and may become, even I, a son of the
day . . . O Merciful One, send the Comforter even to me,
so that He may teach me the things concerning You; and
O God of all, declare what is Yours to me. Illumine me
with the true light, O Compassionate One, so that I may
see the glory which You had with Your Father before the
world was made. Abide even in me, as You have said, so
that I, too, may become worthy of abiding in You, and
may then consciously enter into You and consciously
possess You within myself . . .[10]

The Eastern tradition of spirituality celebrates the uncreated
light of Tabor—the dazzling, healing light of the Transfiguration—
as a key theme titled the *Metamorphosis*. Vladimir Lossky com-
ments: "To see the divine light with bodily sight, as the disciples
saw it on Mount Tabor, we must participate in and be transformed
by it, according to our capacity. Mystical experience implies this
change in our nature, its transformation by grace."[11] Dare we enter the divine light—even participate in the energies of God—if
it might alter us, reshape us, make us different? Symeon the New
Theologian offers this prayer to the Holy Spirit:

You, the gaiety;

You, the mirth;

And Your grace, grace of the Spirit of all sanctity,

Will shine like the sun in all the saints;

And You, inaccessible sun,

will shine in their midst

and all will shine brightly.[12]

In *Hymns of Divine Love* (also called *Hymns of Divine Eros*),
most of which were completed during his time in exile, Symeon

10. Symeon the New Theologian (Golitzin, trans.), *On the Mystical Life*.

11. Lossky, *Mystical Theology*, 223.

12. Symeon the New Theologian, "You O Christ Are the Kingdom of
Heaven," in *Divine Eros*; see also Oliver, *Giver of Life*.

describes his vision of God as uncreated divine light, an experience of divine luminosity. The Hymns recount Symeon's mystical experiences and his love for Christ, which have been described as "ecstatic writing and . . . mystical content that becomes very personal, both to Symeon and to the reader."[13] *Hymn 25* includes the following description of Symeon's mystical union with God as light:

> But, Oh, what intoxication of light, Oh, what movements of fire!
>
> Oh, what swirlings of the flame in me, miserable one that I am,
>
> coming from You and Your glory!
>
> The glory I know it and I say it is Your Holy Spirit,
>
> who has the same nature with You, and the same honor,
>
> O Word;
>
> He is of the same race, the same glory,
>
> of the same essence, He alone with your Father,
>
> and with you, O Christ, O God of the universe!
>
> I fall down in adoration before You.
>
> I thank You that You have made me worthy to know, however
>
> little it may be,
>
> the power of Your divinity.[14]

Reflection: Questions

1. What strikes you most from the Franciscan tradition?

2. How do you find yourself responding to the phrase "the humanity of God"?

3. How do you react to Francis's take on suffering?

4. What questions would you ask Symeon, if you had the chance to meet him?

13. Symeon, the New Theologian (Catanzaro, trans.), *Discourses*, introduction.

14. Symeon the New Theologian (Catanzaro, trans.), *Discourses*, 24.

Experience: Prayer Exercise

Either:

Use the cross prayers devised by Francis of Assisi. Open your arms wide—extend them as far as you can. This is first to embody a solidarity with the cross. Think of Jesus opening wide his arms on the cross to embrace all who suffer, all who are in any form of distress. Think of Christ's all-encompassing love and acceptance. Second, think of the risen Christ and the way he longs to enfold the whole of creation, the little ones and marginalized ones of the earth. Third, offer this prayer as an act of intercession. It is a prayer that hurts—in the sense that your arms will grow weary and ache. Moses prayed like this and had to have others hold his arms up (Exod 17:11,12). As you feel the ache, let it connect you to those who are in pain, those who are hurting: the sick, the dispossessed, those whose human rights are trampled on. Finally, use this prayer-action as an act of self-offering. Offer yourself afresh to God for the part he has in store for you in his mission of reconciliation in the world.

Or:

Practice the Jesus Prayer of Orthodoxy, uniting it to your breath: "Lord Jesus Christ, Son of God" (breathing in divine life) "Have mercy on me, a sinner" (exhaling sinfulness and negativity). Repeat many times, allowing it to sink, as it were, from the head (focusing on the words' meaning) to the heart (allowing it to be united with the heartbeat and pulse of your being).

Further Reading

Brother Ramon, SSF. *Franciscan Spirituality: Following St Francis Today.* London: SPCK, 2008.

Meyendorf, John. *Byzantine Theology.* London: Mowbrays, 1974.

FIGURE 5

5

Through Herod's Gate

Exploring Sufi Worlds

Invitation

HEROD'S GATE LEADS DIRECTLY to the Muslim Quarter and invites us to encounter the Sufi mystical tradition that is represented by the many Sufi buildings in this part of the city. Prior to Friday prayers a tide of humanity funnels into this entry point, already narrowed by fruit sellers' stands. The gate was opened during the Ottoman period in the northern wall, which from the time of Titus's siege in 70 CE has always been the most vulnerable part of the city's defenses, because outside it the land is higher and attackers often arrived from the north. Its name originates from traditions that locate the palace of Herod in this district. Today it is known in Arabic as Bab az Zahra, which derives from the verb "to be watchful," referring not to vigilance about visitors but from the graveyard opposite, reserved for departed pilgrims who have travelled to Mecca, and who await the resurrection on the last day. The word is close to the Arabic word for "blossom," so it is also known as the Flowers Gate.

In the Mamluk period (1187–1517) and Ottoman period (1517–1917) there were seventy Sufi institutions within the walls of Jerusalem. When the great Ottoman traveler Evliya Celebi arrived in the seventeenth century, he wrote: "Jerusalem is the Mecca of the dervishes!" The first Sufis had come to the Holy City in the early centuries of Islam from the eastern provinces of the Islamic world. Marginal figures, well outside the mainstream of public life, they encountered Christian monks and hermits living in the deserts to the east of the city. Like them, the first Sufis were ascetics—wandering, fasting, and retreating to the hills for long vigils of solitary prayer and contemplation.

As they began to attract disciples, drawn by the magnetism of their spiritual experience, they became known as the *awliya*—the friends of God. Distinct Sufi *tariqas*—"paths" or schools of wisdom—began to emerge, each with distinctive styles of worship and particular forms of prayer and practice. Sufi guesthouses and lodges (*zawiya*) opened both as places of prayer and training and as centers for social service, as *tariqas* began to feed the poor, to welcome guests, and to teach the young. Gradually Sufis moved into the mainstream of Islamic life, as is evidenced by the enduring legacy of Sufi institutional buildings in Jerusalem. Today they find themselves once again at the margins, but continuing to witness to a vital strand of Islamic mysticism.[1]

In this chapter we explore the Sufi way of meditation, which includes sacred dance, with the remembrance of God by recitation of the ninety-nine divine names (the way of *dhikr*).[2] We recall Saint Francis's encounter with Islam (1219) and his devotion to the names of God in his composition *Praises of God*.

As soon as we cross the threshold of Herod's Gate, brushing past the fruit sellers with their colorful, overflowing stalls, and ascend a steep flight of steps on our right, we encounter the Indian Hospice. Two noble pillars frame its green door, above

1. This paragraph is indebted to www.sufitrails.ps/.

2. Among Sufi traditions in Jerusalem are the Rifa'iyya order, developed by Shaikh Ahmad ibn Ali al-Rifa'I; the Qadiriyya order, developed by Abedal-Qader al-Jilani; the Maulawiyya order, developed by Mauwlana Jalal al-Din Al-Rumi; the Bastamiyya order, after Abi Yazid Tayfour al-Bastami; the Naqshabandiyya order, established by Baha' al-Din al-Bukhari; and the Shaziliyya Yashrutiyya order, established by Ali Nour al-Din al-Yashruti.

which an inscription in Arabic announces: *Zawiya al-Hindiya.* This ancient Sufi center was founded by Indian dervish Baba Farid (1173–1266), a founder of the Chishti order of Sufis, a mystical brotherhood that still flourishes today across India, Pakistan, and Afghanistan. Baba Farid walked into Jerusalem around the year 1200, little more than a decade after the armies of Saladin had forced the Crusaders out of Jerusalem. Fasting for forty days in an underground room, he introduced to Jerusalem a distinctive flavor of Sufi mysticism. Some accounts tell us that he spent his days sweeping the stone floors around Al-Aqsa Mosque, or fasting in the silence of a cave inside the city walls. We will consider the ideas of Baba Farid below. Today the Indian flag still flies over this ancient building, which serves as a lodge for Muslim pilgrims from South Asia: Indian Muslims passing through Jerusalem on their way to Mecca want to pray where he had prayed, to sleep where he had slept.[3] Today Sheikh Mohammed Munir Ansari, in his eighties, continues to look after this ancient holy place, aided by his son Nazeer.

The path leads us down via several flights of steps towards the Noble Sanctuary—Haram al Sharif, as Muslims call the Temple Mount. There, of course, the Dome of the Rock and Al-Aqsa Mosque recall the Prophet Muhammad's ascent to heaven during his miraculous night journey, in which he prays with Abraham and Jesus. This ascension represents for Sufi mystics the intersection between a horizontal journey, coming to Jerusalem, and the vertical journey, meeting God, a symbol of the ascent of the soul to the Divine. Mohammed had first—physically or mystically— traveled from Mecca to Jerusalem on his mighty steed, and then experienced a night journey to heaven. There the Prophet received the command to pray—*salat*—to offer prayer five times a day, one of the pillars of Islam. Mohamed's ascension from the Rock, passing through the seven heavens to the divine throne, endures as a paradigm of the Sufi mystical experience of humanity's return to

---

3. See Adamson, "Jerusalem's 800-year-old Indian Hospice."
Until 1948 there were about fifteen resident dervishes at the Indian hospice, drawn from Asian countries.

God: as he loses himself in ecstasy before God, denying his ego and opening himself up to God, so the Sufi is beckoned towards such an ascent of the soul. As Jerusalem became the third holiest Islamic shrine in the world, Sufi institutions—hostels and teaching centers—clustered around the western edges of the Al-Aqsa compound, so people could learn and pray within sight of the Dome, which itself represented the indissoluble unity of God.

Encounter

Soon we reach the Via Dolorosa, the Way of the Cross, and encounter by the Ecce Homo Arch the Naqshbandi Mosque, which preserves ancient Sufi writings. A nearby street is called Aqabat Darwish—*dervish* means "door" in Persian—one who is at the threshold—between the human and divine. A green door leads to a hidden and remarkable world. This is the mosque of the Uzbek community, home to a Muslim congregation representing the Naqshbandi, a major Sufi order with a spiritual lineage going back to Baha-ud-Din Bukhari (1318–1389) of Turkestan. The identity Naqshbandi derives from two ideas: *naqsh*, which means "engraving" (the name of God in the believer's heart), and "band" (meaning "bond," indicating the link between the individual and the Creator.[4] The founder's descendants from Uzbekistan still live in the house on top of the mosque.

Hala is the widow of Sheikh Abdul Aziz Bukhari, a direct descendent of a ninth-century Sunni scholar, whose family came to live in this house in 1616. Sheikh Bukhari was a gentle and irenic man who brought Jew and Palestinian together in real encounter through an interfaith group called the Jerusalem Peacemakers. Often opposed for his bighearted reaching out to others across

4. Islamic scholar Nizami observes: "Spiritually, the Naqshbandiyyah stand out in visualizing a whole universe of spiritual experience and adventure. They have laid out with great conceptual clarity a world of spiritual development indicating the stages and stations through which a mystic adventurer has to pass. Perhaps no other Sufi order has ever attempted this task so meticulously." Nizami, "The Naqshbandiyyah Order."

divides, it was the stress and tension he faced through this work, it is said, that triggered his heart attack and tragic death in June 2011. But his widow is determined to carry on his vital task of reconciliation.

Hala welcomes me to her home. From its terrace you can see the golden Dome of the Rock glistening in the sun. Inside, her flat is filled with display cases preserving the great collection of ancient handwritten Islamic texts which her husband had assembled over many years. On the wall is a certificate, proudly displayed: it celebrates her role in the Women's Federation for World Peace, giving thanks for her as an "ambassador for peace." She is involved in bringing together women from different sides of the conflict in Israel/Palestine. She is a healing presence, and knows there are many wounds to be healed. She explains her vision of Sufi spirituality:[5]

> My husband could see that there is only one God and we are all his children. It is as simple as that. Why make it any more complicated? In this land, we are also all children of Abraham. He is our common father and prophet. We need to relate to each other with our hearts. We need to reach out to each other with our hands. We need to look at each other with open, trusting eyes. We need to understand one another with our minds. As a Sufi community we meet every Thursday for the dhikr: the remembrance of God, achieved by the recital of the beautiful names of Allah. We chant Allah, Allah, Allah, adding the beautiful Name each time. We feel his presence with us. But most of all, we pray that the Name will become part of us, that we will become more like God, more compassionate, more forgiving. So the divine nature grows in our human nature. That is the aim. That is what we are called to. The Sufi way has much to teach us about the path to peace.
>
> My husband started the Jerusalem Hug. Every summer thousands of local residents and visitors encircle the whole walled city of Jerusalem with a hug. We experience

63

and express what peace is, as we join hands across the cultures and make one circle. Musicians, singers, dancers, artists, and healers come from many places around the world to take part. This human chain around the walls of the Old City symbolizes our hopes for Jerusalem. What we need to do most in this city is build relationships, build true community.

Mohammed is a local shopkeeper and visits the Naqshbandi mosque several times during the day. He explains to me a little of his practice:

> When I pray I use my body. I turn my head to the left, chin on the shoulder and I say: "Peace be to you brothers and angels in the east." Then I turn my head to the right and say "Peace be to you brothers and angels in the west." I do this again and again. From our prayer comes peace to the world.

In the block behind we encounter the Afghan mosque, established in 1603, where every Thursday evening the *dhikr* dancing and chanting are celebrated.[6] Al-Qadiriyya is named after the dignified scholar Sheikh Abed al Qader al-Jilani, the founder and pioneer of the Qadiri Sufi order in the Islamic world. Built by Muhammad Pasha, governor of Jerusalem, this *zawiya* is currently known as the Afghaniyya, due to a number of Afghanis residing in it. The Shadhili order cares for this center with imam Sheikh Abdul-Karim al-Afghani.

Towards the sacred enclosure of Al- Aqsa Mosque, one can seek out the former Sufi center of Al-Ribat Al-Mansuri, now home to the Afro-Palestinian community.[7] Further down we encounter

6. To visit al-Qadiriyya, backtrack to Mujahidin Street and walk towards al-Wad Street. Turn left at Barquq Street and walk a few dozen meters to the southern corner of al-Zawiya al-Qadiriyya.

7. From the main thoroughfare al-Wad Street, walk until Al-Nzhir Gate crossing and Aqabat al-Takiyya, then turn left and walk until just before Bab-al-Nazhir Gate leading to al-Aqsa Mosque. The Ribat is located at the southern side of Bab al-Nazir, across from Ala al-Din Al-Basir Ribat. It is possible to visit al-Ribat's facilities, including the main hall and the entrance. Residents of al-Ribat are particularly friendly and welcoming.

the Khanqa al-Dawadariyya, near the Haram or Temple Mount, dating from 1295.[8] This is a Khan, or hospice for pilgrims: its inscription above the entrance indicates that it was established in an effort to please Allah, and to provide shelter to thirty members of Arab and non-Arab members of the Sufi order. Any Sufi arriving at the Khan would be hosted for a period of ten days. Al-Dawadariyya is noted for the beauty of its architectural details—built from interlocking red and grey stones. The inscription is marked with three rows of beautifully formed stalactite stone elements, while above the entrance a pointed arch is fashioned from colorful stones. The entrance leads directly to an open, rectangular paved courtyard, surrounded from the north and south by rooms where Sufi pilgrims stay. A large rectangular hall is used for teaching the Qur'an and Hadith, and for Sufi meditations.

As we approach the most sacred part of the Holy City for Muslims, the Noble Sanctuary, we recall the evocative nighttime description by seventeenth-century pilgrim Celebri:

> All along the southern, western, and northern side of the Haram enclosures are porticoes with domes, resting over three hundred and sixty columns. All porticoes are lit every night by oil lamps. They become as bright as broad daylight. In these porticoes live dervishes from India, Sind, Balkh, Persia; and Kurds, Tartars, Moghuls, and Turks. They need by night no special candles, for the oil lamps give out so much light that they can read the Qur'an and recite the *zikr* and offer God the best prayers.[9]

What is the practice of Sufi prayer here today? We meet Islamic scholar and inspector of the Al-Aqsa Mosque, Sheikh Mazen Ahram.[10] Sheikh Ahram, a kindly man in his sixties and deeply respected across Jerusalem, tells me:

8. The al-Dawadariyya is located directly south of the Salamiyya School, on Bab al-Atm Street, and adjacent to al-Aqsa Mosque from the north.

9. Quoted in Sarna, *Indians at Herod's Gate*, 118.

10. I am grateful to distinguished Jerusalem anthropologist Dr. Ali Qleibo and to Wajeeh Nuseibeh, Muslim keeper of the keys to the Holy Sepulcher, for helping to facilitate this meeting. Sheikh Mazen Ahram (inspector of the Al-Aqsa Mosque), interview by Andrew Mayes in June 2014 at St George's

My family arrived in Jerusalem with the Caliph Omar. I am descended thirty-nine generations from the Prophet, peace be upon him. We have resided in the holy city for thirteen generations. I have worked at the Waqf [the Islamic body that governs the Noble Sanctuary] for forty years and oversee a hundred mosques in Jerusalem. As a Sufi, I seek peace between the religions.

Every hundred years God sends a teacher to instruct his people. The teacher for this generation is Ahmad Al-Alawi, who died fifty years ago, and I am influenced by him and his principal student, Mustafa. The sheikh entrusted to Mustafa the task of continuing his teaching. There is an unbroken continuity through time—we are all part of one family, all brothers, with a precious link through the generations.

Our *zawiya* meets in a part of the Al-Aqsa Mosque. Sufis are interested in regular religious practices but the key aim is to draw the Name of God into the heart. We are interested in the big questions . . . a knowledge of humanity; why are we here? We enter the door of belief—seeking to understand God, prayer, the last day, good and evil. Most of all we believe that everything comes from God.

There are three stages in the spiritual path.

We begin with *islam*—surrender of our life to God, following the external practices. Then we progress to *iman* where fear turns to love, and our practice becomes more interior, in the heart. But we are aiming at *ihsan*. We begin to get a feeling of God. We follow the way of God. We realize that God sees everything. He looks into the heart. We keep hope all the time, mindful of God in whatever we are doing, whether working or whatever. God watches me, eating or fasting . . . The divine names we recite become part of us; they get inside of us.

Our *dhikr* celebrations are in three parts.

First, we read a chapter from the Holy Qur'an. The sheikh explains the text and in his sermon gets to the meaning of it, as we sit in a circle. We are asking: what is this saying to our lives?

College in Jerusalem.

Second, there is the *Wird*—it means "access"—a time of preparation for access to the Divine. This is the singing.

Third comes the most important stage, the calling of the divine name. There are movements of the body to correspond with four letters of the divine name Allah. We open our eyes and as it were we see the Name of Allah before us. Then we close the eyes and we can still see the Name imprinted on our consciousness. As we repeat the Name we take a short intake of breath on the last part of the Name, the letter *Ha*, to get the *Ha* into our heart.

We stand in a circle, joining hands. We don't dance like the Whirling Dervishes, or have flutes. That could distract us. We want to concentrate on the Name of Allah. If we have prepared ourselves, washed and cleansed, we will be receptive. As we recite God's Name we are reborn in the road to Allah. Our hearts become full of mercy, love, and giving. As our revered teacher Raba'a of the Mount of Olives taught, "If my heart is full of love, there is no place for hate." The key feeling, as I said, is to love God and to be filled with love, and to carry this into our daily life. The people who fight in the streets need to get this knowledge. Hate blocks. Love opens. And we can practice *dhikr*, the remembrance of God, all the time. When we see a flower, or even a cat (there are a lot of cats in Jerusalem!), we practice *dhikr* and remember Allah.

We don't judge; we don't punish. We live in peace. You see, the ceremony in the mosque leads to life in the world; it leads to peace, rest, respect. We drink in the mercy, like a baby on the breast. We drink in God, feel his warmth, know our dependence on him like an infant in the arms of his mother.

Allah has taught us seven steps.

We begin by realizing we do bad things, feel sorrow for that, seek forgiveness. We start to recognize the problem of the ego or self-indulgence.

Then we choose to enter again in the right way, hearing the voice of conscience and resisting carnal desires.

Next, I work with my heart to do right things, with my mind to do good things.

I reach a safe state, I feel comfortable.

At the fifth stage, I remind myself that I receive everything from God, both the good things and the bad things. I reach a state of satisfaction and contentment as I receive all things from God, and start to gain the divine attributes.

Reaching the final stage—I cannot tell you about this. The soul is a secret from God, no one knows about it. Like the mystery of Gabriel coming to Mohammed, peace be upon him, at Mecca. I know this: the soul goes on forever, but the body falls to dust. The soul filled with God's mercy is like electric light being switched on in a house, it brightens everything up!

The Holy Qur'an teaches us that there are different parts to the human: the *nafs* (the self); the heart (desiring God); the secret soul, of which I cannot speak. But this thing is sure: If we know ourselves, we know God.

Reciting the divine names or attributes makes us close to God, even to have an affinity with God. And it makes us want to make this troubled land a place of peace.

As Sheikh Ahram leaves, his eyes delight on flowers and the first buds of spring. He spontaneously exults: "God is in this bud!" And as he turns to reenter the hustle and bustle of the streets, with a twinkle in his eye he calls out: "You can practice *dhikr*, the remembrance of God *wherever* you go!"

Discovery

We encounter three of the greatest Sufi mystics associated with Jerusalem: Raba'a, Baba Farid, and Rumi.

Raba'a

Sheikh Ahram referred to Raba'a, the great female Sufi mystic, whose tomb stands next to the Mosque of the Ascension atop the Mount of Olives. Born in the Iraqi city of Basra in 713, she crossed the deserts to reach Jerusalem. A Sufi poet, singer, and mystic,

Raba'a pioneered the daring use of the language of intimacy for the Divine, famously developed by Rumi. God was for her the only Beloved. Stunningly beautiful herself and frequently pursued by would-be lovers, she consecrated herself, body and soul, to God. She was enslaved until the man who purchased her saw light radiating around her one evening while she was kneeling in prayer. Raba'a wrote poems describing her unquenchable love for God. Her spiritual love was referred to as adoration (in Arabic, *ashq*). Camille Adams Helminski explains her significance:

> As the mystical side of Islam developed, it was a woman who first expressed the relationship with the Divine in a language we have come to recognize as specifically Sufic by referring to God as the Beloved. Raba'a was the first human being to speak of the realities of Sufism with a language that anyone could understand. Though she experienced many difficulties in her early years, Raba'a's starting point was neither a fear of hell nor a desire for paradise, but only love. "God is God," she said—"for this I love God . . . not because of any gifts, but for itself." Her aim was to melt her being in God. According to her, one could find God by turning within oneself.[11]

Let's listen to her voice singing across the centuries:

> O God, the stars are shining;
> All eyes have closed in sleep:
> The kings have locked their doors.
> Each lover is alone, in secret, with the one he loves.
> And I am here too: hidden from all of them—
> With You[12]

> How long will you keep pounding an open door
> Begging for someone to open it?[13]

---

11. Helminski, *Women of Sufism*.
12 Upton, trans., *Doorkeeper of the Heart*, 66.
13. Upton, trans., *Doorkeeper of the Heart*, 63.

. . . lift the veil

And let me feast my eyes on Your Living Face.[14]

In love, nothing exists between breast and Breast.

Speech is born out of longing.

True description from the real taste.

The one who tastes, knows;

The one who explains, lies.[15]

O God,

Whenever I listen to the voice of anything You have made—

The rustling of the trees

The trickling of water

The cries of birds

The flickering of shadow

The roar of the wind

The song of the thunder—

I hear it saying:

God is One!

Nothing can be compared with God![16]

Raba'a composes a new list of divine names:

My joy

My hunger

My shelter

My friend

My food for the journey

My journey's end

You are my breath,

My hope,

14. Upton, trans., *Doorkeeper of the Heart*, 6.

15. Upton, trans., *Doorkeeper of the Heart*, 31.

16. Upton, trans., *Doorkeeper of the Heart*, 58.

My companion,
My craving,
My abundant wealth . . .
My life, my love . . .
O captain of my heart,
Radiant eye of yearning in my breast . . .
Be satisfied with me, Love
And I am satisfied[17]

Referring to the practice of the remembrance of God she writes,

Your hope in my heart is the rarest treasure
Your Name on my tongue is the sweetest word
My choicest hours
Are the hours I spend with You—

O God, I can't live in this world
Without remembering You—[18]

Give the goods of this world to Your enemies—
Give the treasures of Paradise to Your friends—
But as for me—You are all I need.

O God!
If I adore You out of fear of Hell, burn me in Hell!
If I adore You out of desire for Paradise,
Lock me out of Paradise.
But if I adore You for Yourself alone,
Do not deny to me Your eternal beauty[19]

17. Upton, trans., *Doorkeeper of the Heart*, 57.
18. Upton, trans., *Doorkeeper of the Heart*, 51.
19. Upton, trans., *Doorkeeper of the Heart*, 47.

Baba Farid

The Indian Hospice, which greets us as soon as we cross the threshold of Herod's Gate, introduces us to the spirituality of Baba Farid (1173–1266), known as the father of Punjabi poetry and revered as one of the most distinguished Muslim mystics of the medieval period. His remarkable poetry was to influence the Sikh religion; many of his sayings were incorporated into the Sikh holy text, the Guru Granth, and the Sikh founder, Guru Nanak, was inspired by his teaching.

Farid writes of a gateway to the Divine:

> All those that He is gathering, dervishes at His door are becoming...[20]

At God's door the soul must unburden itself as it comes into the divine presence:

> It is a difficult job, to at the door of God be a beggar...
> How to get rid of an albatross, the load that I wear?...[21]
> Path of God's love is difficult, for fruit of past deeds
> One carries on head, no matter how heavy load is,
>   or one's needs[22]

There must be a relinquishment of the baggage one carries, a radical letting go, if we seek the Divine. There must be an honesty, too:

> Farid, rip off silk veil, your rough woolen cloak be wearing:
> To meet the Beloved... wear what is natural to be wearing.[23]

He images the Divine as an ocean to be explored, and we should not be content with the shallows:

> You've to fathom the ocean, it has what you're wanting!

20. Smith, trans., *Baba Farid*, 60.
21. Smith, trans., *Baba Farid*, 110.
22. Smith, trans., *Baba Farid*, 78.
23. Smith, trans., *Baba Farid*, 49.

Why with your hands sail the small ponds for what you're
searching?[24]

A key theme is that the heart is the locus of the Divine. Farid ex-
plores the paradox between a keen sense of human mortality, des-
tined for dust, and humanity's astonishing capacity for the Divine:

> Why roam the jungle with thorns pricking your feet?
> Your Lord is in your heart, you wander hoping Him you'll meet![25]
> Don't look in wilderness or to a bed of thorns take . . .
> That One isn't outside, in your heart is One, awake![26]

But the heart must be tamed, disciplined:

> Farid, today is the day of union, it's the time to be taming
> the wild cranes of desire the heart are inciting, are inflaming.[27]

> Fire that in heart secretly burns, reason can't see . . .
> Search in your heart, look down, try to be true.[28]

> In every heart God's living, so don't hurt any heart . . .
> each is a precious gem: don't be breaking any heart![29]

Farid urges us to a life of simplicity and contentment in ba-
sics. There is no place for envy or covetousness:

> With just simple bread and cool water be satisfied . . .
> by the tasty food of others do not ever be tempted . . .[30]
> O Farid, eat your own dry bread, drink plain cold water:
> seeing another's buttered bread, do not let mind wander![31]

24. Smith, trans., *Baba Farid*, 52.
25. Smith, trans., *Baba Farid*, 50.
26. Smith, trans., *Baba Farid*, 118.
27. Smith, trans., *Baba Farid*, 67.
28. Smith, trans., *Baba Farid*, 114.
29. Smith, trans., *Baba Farid*, 138.
30. Smith, trans., *Baba Farid*, 120.
31. Smith, trans., *Baba Farid*, 89.

In the spiritual life there may be a place for ritual and dance. But God is not limited:

> His grace may fall on us at anytime, it has no rules . . . you see?
> Some don't get it after rituals, vigils: others asleep,
>   it hits suddenly![32]

Above all, for Farid life is a quest for the Beloved, for an elusive intimacy with the Divine:

> Last night I was sad, afterwards of my beautiful Love I thought
> . . .
> I said I'd do all to get to Him: tears ran . . .sleeve, My Lover caught.[33]

Rumi

In the heart of the Muslim Quarter, we stumble on the hard-to-find Maylawiyya *zawiya* established in the year 1543 CE by the Ottoman governor of Jerusalem, which preserves the memory and tradition of Jamaluddin Rumi (b. 1207), the best-known Sufi poet in the West. The Ottoman sultans gave special honor to the sheikhs and followers of the Maylawiyya Tariqa (*tariqa* = religious path or religious order), which Rumi founded. Sultan Salim appointed Akhfash Zada as the sheikh of Rumi's Tariqa in Jerusalem, and he ordered his government to endow it generously. The *zawiya* includes a large courtyard, which has witnessed generations of Sufi dancing, poetry, and music in Rumi's tradition.

Rumi has popularized the Sufi tradition of calling prayer "a path of love," where the Sufi becomes the "lover" and God the "Beloved." This love affair ends only with the ultimate union with the Beloved. This love relationship is depicted in most volumes of Sufi literature and poetry, but Rumi gives clearest expression to it

---

32. Smith, trans., *Baba Farid*, 62.
33. Smith, trans., *Baba Farid*, 40.

through his sensuous language. He describes the true Sufi in these terms:

> What makes the Sufi? Purity of heart; Not the patched mantle
>
> . . .
>
> He in all dregs discerns the essence pure:
> In hardship ease, in tribulation joy.[34]

> We are the flute, our music is all Yours;
> We are the mountains echoing only You
> And move to defeat or victory;
> Lions emblazoned high on flags unfurled-
> Your wind invisible sweeps us through the world.[35]

Evoking Mohammed's night journey and entry into heaven from the site we call the Dome of the Rock, when the Prophet was given the divine summons to *salat,* prayer, Rumi writes of the ascent of the soul in the experience of prayer:

> At every instant and from every side, resounds the call of Love:
> We are going to sky, who wants to come with us?
> We have gone to heaven, we have been the friends of the angels,
> And now we will go back there, for there is our country.
> We are higher than heaven, more noble than the angels:
> Why not go beyond them? Our goal is the Supreme Majesty.
> What has the fine pearl to do with the world of dust?
> Why have you come down here? Take your baggage back.
>   What is this place?
> Luck is with us, to us is the sacrifice! . . .

> Like the birds of the sea, men come from the ocean—the ocean
>   of the soul.

34. Arberry, ed., *Persian Poems,* "The True Sufi."

35. "The Unseen Power" translated by Reynold A. Nicholson in Arberry, *Persian Poems.*

> How could this bird, born from that sea, make his dwelling
>   here?
> No, we are the pearls from the bosom of the sea, it is there that
>   we dwell:
> Otherwise how could the wave succeed to the wave that comes
>   from the soul?
> The wave named "Am I not your Lord" has come; it has broken
>   the vessel of the body;
> And when the vessel is broken, the vision comes back, and the
>   union with Him.[36]

Rumi likens the soul to a soaring bird:

> At last thou hast departed and gone to the Unseen;
> 'Tis marvellous by what way thou went from the world.
> Thou didst strongly shake thy wings and feathers,
> and having broken thy cage
> Didst take to the air and journey towards the world of Soul.
> Thou wert a favorite falcon, kept in captivity by an old woman:
> When thou heard the falcon-drum thou didst fly away into the
>   Void.
> Thou wert a love-lorn nightingale among owls:
> The scent of the Rose-Garden, reached thee,
> and thou didst go to the Rose-Garden.[37]

Encountering the Other: Francis and the Sultan

The first Sufi institution established by Saladin in 1187 is located
just off Saint Francis Street in the Christian Quarter: the original
building stands, serving as a Muslim residence. Its location by
Saint Francis Street prompts us to recall Saint Francis's extraordinary encounter with Islam. Sultan Malek al Kamil recognized him
as a mystic because he was dressed in brown robes just like the

36. Quoted in Vitray-Meyerovitch, *Rumi and Sufism*, n.p.
37. Quoted in Davis, *Persian Mystics*, n.p.

revered Sufis of the time. The encounter taught Francis the value of the sacred names, which he adopted in his own litany.

This exchange took place in the midst of war. In 1219 Christian knights of the Fifth Crusade besieged the city of Damietta on the Nile delta, an important entry point for pilgrims traveling towards the Holy Land. The Crusaders' mission was to open up the routes of pilgrimage to the Church of the Resurrection, which were in Muslim hands. Their strategy was the way of violence: they aimed to slaughter as many followers of Islam as they could. When Francis arrived in Damietta, he tried to dissuade the Crusaders from their bloody action, but nobody listened. So, accompanied by one brother, Illuminato, Francis crossed the battle lines.

First he left the relative safety of the crusader military camp. Francis had to step into no-man's land that separated the warring factions and, in order to reach the enemy camp, had to traverse forbidding defensive ditches and heavily armed enemy barriers. On reaching the city of Damietta, he fearlessly crossed three walls. His aim was to reach the sultan of Egypt himself, Malek al Kamil, nephew of Saladin the Great, who had taken Jerusalem in 1187. Saint Francis was turned back at every point, but was resolute and somehow got past the soldiers guarding the walls that kept the two camps apart.

He succeeded in having an extended dialogue with the sultan, who received him with deep respect. For his part, Francis saw the sultan as a brother, and in the process he learned a great deal about the foreign world of Islam, glimpsing new perspectives on "the infidel religion," which had been viewed in the West through the eyes of prejudice and fear. Francis was changed by this meeting, and it left an abiding mark on his own spirituality. The litany on the divine names, *The Praises of God*, which he composed later, after receiving the stigmata at Mount La Verna, looks like a meditation on the Islamic ninety-nine names of God: "You are the holy Lord. God . . . You are strong. You are great. You are the most high. You are the almighty king . . . You are the good, all good, the highest Good."[38]

38. Quoted in Armstrong et al., eds., *Francis of Assisi*, 1:109.

In the event at Damietta, Francis emerges as an intrepid and audacious risk-taker, energized by the love of Christ, as he breaches the walls that divided two peoples. His encounter with the sultan is sometimes considered the first example of genuine Christian–Islamic dialogue. Certainly it has inspired many to realize how walls can be breached.

Reflection: Questions

1. What lines from Raba'a, Rumi, or Baba Farid strike you most? Why?

2. Can you think of any parallels in your tradition that resonate with these words?

3. How do you feel about using the language of intimacy with God? Are you comfortable or uncomfortable about this? Why?

4. What feelings arise in you when you use this sort of language in prayer? What effect does it have on you?

5. The Sufis were well known for their dancing and rhythmic movements in prayer. How do you bring your own body into prayer?

Experience: Prayer Exercise

Compose your own litany of divine names using startling images and metaphors that spring from the heart's experience.

Or:

Write a poem, or a love letter to God expressing your heart's desire.

Further Reading

Kabbani, Muhammad Hisham. *The Naqshbandi Sufi Tradition Guidebook of Daily Practices and Devotions*. Washington, DC: Islamic Supreme Council of America, 2004.

Douglas-Klotz, Neil. *The Sufi Book of Life: 99 Pathways of the Heart for the Modern Dervish*. New York: Penguin Compass, 2005.

Frager, Robert, and James Frager, eds. *Essential Sufism*. San Francisco: HarperSanFrancisco, 1997.

Lings, Martin. *What Is Sufism?* Cambridge: Islamic Texts Society, 1993.

FIGURE 6

6

Through the Lions' Gate

Walking the Way of the Cross

THE LIONS' GATE IS named after the ferocious animal carvings on it—actually tigers or leopards stare down from the walls, being the heraldic symbol of thirteenth-century Sultan Baybars, who had a lifelong struggle against the Crusaders. This gateway leads us directly to the uphill path of the Via Dolorosa, the Way of the Cross, which runs like a secret river through the very center of the Holy City. Interviews with locals in this chapter will help us realize how the *Way of the Cross* is a very contemporary devotion, with poignant resonances today.

The most famous road in the Christian imagination, the Way of the Cross, the Via Dolorosa, is depicted on the walls of thousands of churches worldwide—after the Franciscans in the fourteen century popularized the devotion, and parish churches provided pictorial representations in the form of the stations of the cross, for those who could not go on pilgrimage to Jerusalem. Today the Way of the Cross remains the most popular Lenten devotion and has spread beyond the Catholic Church to be adopted by a wide array of reformed churches. Indeed, churches of all denominations often join together in walking the Way of the Cross on Good Friday, as an open-air ecumenical act of witness in cities and towns everywhere.

Sometimes people are tempted to transform this into something too narrowly devotional, an individualistic matter between "me and my Lord," disconnected from contemporary realities in the wider world. Another risk of observing the stations of the cross is that the devotion might become merely an act of historical remembrance, as if marking only a faraway event, unrelated to the present. But there is a great opportunity to rediscover the Way of the Cross as one of the most powerful forms of intercession there is, as we allow it to lead us into prayerful solidarity with those who suffer on the face of the earth. Here we meet those who actually live on the physical Via Dolorosa in Jerusalem today. It is a road marked by paradox. It is marked by heartache and hope, by desperation and ideology, by failure and promise. It is a street of anguish and aspirations, of witness and denial, of brokenness and healing, of trauma and peace. It is certainly a road of passion today—in the sense that people experience both great suffering and intense human emotions.

In this chapter we notice how prayer and pain blend, how hope and fears meet as we listen to the voices of those who live on the Way of the Cross today—and feel the pulse and heartbeat of the living city. These are voices of passion and hope—sometimes shocking or disturbing, sometimes revealing extraordinary courage and faith—reflecting the contemporary context for an ancient devotion.

Jesus walks the Way of the Cross not as one solitary individual from Nazareth, but as the new Adam, as everyman/everywoman, a corporate universal figure who gathers into himself the pain of the ages. As Suffering Servant he gathered unto himself the hopes and griefs of all people: "Surely he has borne our infirmities and carried our diseases" (Isa 53:4). As Son of Man, he bears the pain of humanity. And Matthew 25 invites us to look today for the features of Christ in the faces of those who suffer, to be alert to his presence in those who are hurting.

Even in the New Testament we get the sense that Jesus is suffering still, after his resurrection. To Saul, the risen Christ says: "I am Jesus and you are persecuting me" (Acts 9:5). The writer of

Colossians speaks of his sufferings: "in my flesh I complete what is lacking in Christ's afflictions for the sake of his body, that is, his church" (Col 1:12). The Letter to the Hebrews suggests that it is possible to crucify Christ afresh (Heb 6:6). Pascal wrote: "Christ is in agony until the end of time." In our very midst he suffers and rises today. Today he falls down into the dirt and dust in the experience of those whose human rights are trampled upon.

This has particular resonance in the Holy Land. As Naim Ateek puts it, "For Palestinian Christians, the experience of Golgotha is not a distant past or sad memory; it is part of everyday indignity and oppression. Our *Via Dolorosa* is not a mere ritualistic procession through the narrow streets of the old city of Jerusalem but the fate of being subjugated and humiliated in our own land."[1]

It is significant that the Via Dolorosa winds its way through the very center of the Old City of Jerusalem today. It begins at the northern edge of the Temple Mount, with all its Jewish associations and memories and at the selfsame moment it begins in the Muslim Quarter with its present sadnesses. At points it is crossed by Jewish Orthodox hurrying down to prayer at the Western Wall, and at the same time it witnesses Muslim men kneeling on their mats at the time of prayer in their shops. It passes a place for the rehabilitation of blind refugees and others with disabilities. Along its route today are found soldiers, beggars, pilgrims, and tourists; street sellers, laughing children, and disabled elderly. This river of prayer and passion flows in the broken heart of the city, as a potential source of healing and forgiveness. Just as human characters of old were caught up into its drama and flow—Mary, Simon of Cyrene, Veronica, the weeping women—so today the Way of the Cross gathers into itself the joys and pains of the residents of the city who are going about their daily round.

Thus one can walk this way and pray this way as an act of solidarity and in recognition of human trauma today. In prayer one seeks the gift of empathy that one may glimpse, however faintly, that the Way of the Cross is a present reality across the world. We seek the gift of *compassion*—the word literally means "suffering

1. Ateek, *Contemporary Way of the Cross.*

with." Thus the Way of the Cross can become for us not only an act of intercession for all who find themselves treading a path of pain today, wherever in the world, but also an act of solidarity with all Christ's wounded and rising brothers and sisters.

Clowning and Hurting:
The Children of the Via Dolorosa

Station 1 recalls where Jesus is judged by Pilate. Down the road, at the city gate, we recall the cries of children greeting Jesus on his Palm Sunday entry into the Holy City, the children playfully, and mischievously perhaps, pulling down palm branches to wave at the Messiah (Matt 21: 6–11). Today, arising from the massive rock which once served as the foundation for Pontius Pilate's Antonia Fortress, myriad children's voices fill the air once more. Today, where the Roman citadel built by Herod the Great once overlooked the Temple Mount, the Omariyya Boys' School stands proudly. The school owes its name to a noble moment in Jerusalem's history: it means "the covenant of Omar." When the Muslim caliph conquered Jerusalem in 637, he granted to Patriarch Sophronius freedom of worship and noninference with the shrine of the Resurrection, a stunning gesture of respect and tolerance toward the Other. Mohammed, the school gatekeeper, tells me that today 950 children study here, from the age of six to twelve years. Half come from the Old City itself, and half from Arab villages neighboring Jerusalem. The Arab population is young: the United Nations reports that Youth (aged fifteen to twenty-nine) compose thirty percent of the total Palestinian population, and all children and youth under the age of twenty-nine make up over fifty percent of the population.[2] Their cheerful voices nevertheless reveal hidden traumas. Eighty-one percent of Arab children in Jerusalem live below the poverty line (as do 36 percent of Jewish children).[3] They live in desperately overcrowded apartments, where they are

2. United Nations, United Nations Population Fund, "Young People" (https://palestine.unfpa.org/en/node/22580).

3. Association for Civil Rights in Israel, "East Jerusalem—Facts and Figures."

exposed to the adult world at an early point, and domestic violence is sometimes an expression of simmering frustration and anger at intolerable and unending stress in the city. Many have been traumatized by seeing firsthand acts of political violence. The unremitting tensions in the Old City, which occasionally peak into street violence, take their toll on the children as they grow up.

Schoolchildren look out from their classrooms on the sublime site of the majestic Dome of the Rock, across the Haram al Sharif, the Noble Sanctuary. The octagonal building crowned with the vast golden dome was built in 691 to protect the mighty rock of Mount Moriah, the highest peak of the Ophel ridge and the original Canaanite high place of the city of Salem from perhaps the third millennium BCE. Underneath the school Israeli scholars have excavated a controversial subterranean tunnel that exposes the entire length of the Western Wall, with its massive Herodian blocks, each weighing many tons. The tunnel was cut directly beneath the Muslim homes overhead, causing subsidence and disrupting water supplies. When it was opened, it triggered bitter clashes between Muslim residents and Israeli soldiers, resulting in injuries and deaths. The tunnel makes its exit right under the access stairs to the school so that the children pass its armed security guards every day as they ascend the stairs to class. As children stream out of school at the end of the day, so from a door beneath their flight of school steps emerge Jewish visitors, having completed their underground tour, both groups spilling simultaneously onto the Via Dolorosa.

Dr. Jantien Dajani, director of the nearby Spafford Children's Center, tells me:[4]

> There is a desperate shortage of school places for children. There are five thousand children of school age out of school in the Old City and East Jerusalem. At night, the children live on the street. By day the Via Dolorosa is crowded with pilgrims, but in the evening it is transformed: it becomes a playground, football pitch,

4. Dr. Jantien Dajani (director of Spafford Children's Center), interview by Andrew Mayes in October 2010.

and cycle track! But one thing I have noticed about the children is how violent their play can be—pushing, screaming, cursing each other—kicking is the favorite way of expressing yourself. Their play can be aggressive and spiteful. They bully each other sometimes. Guns are a favorite toy, even for the girls.

There seems to be a cycle of violence. Children pick up stress from their parents, who may be unemployed or desperately poor. Their flats will be impossibly crowded: maybe ten to a room. And there is a spiral of fear. Parents are well aware of the stresses of living under military occupation, and they pass this onto the children.

The tribal society of the Old City does have advantages. There is none of the isolation or loneliness children can feel in the West, where each home is behind its fence. Here it is life together, a close community, children in and out of each other's homes. We must not forget the childhood joys. Families are loving, and we hear children laughing and joking—they are not aware that they live under occupation. For them it is normal.

Station 2 marks where Jesus receives his cross. The Sisters of Our Lady of Zion came here in 1856, establishing a convent and school above a substantial stretch of Roman flagstones, which was identified for many years as the Gabbatha pavement or the *lithostrotos* where Pilate gave judgment (John 19:13). The Ecce Homo Arch, which spans the street here, traditionally marks the place where Pilate offered Jesus back to the crowd with the words: "Behold the man!" (John 19:5).

Led by their founder Father Theodore Ratisbonne, the first mission of the sisters was to convert Jews. But everything changed during the Second World War. The sisters found themselves in Germany hiding and protecting Jewish children as the Holocaust unfolded. They asked: How can such things happen in Christian Europe? The Second Vatican Council's 1965 document *Nostra Aetate* (The Relation of the Church to Non-Christian Religions) opened up new perspectives for interreligious dialogue, and today the sisters help facilitate face-to-face meetings between Christians and Jews and teach biblical studies with a focus on Jewish sources.

From the rooftop of the convent the cityscape panorama unfolds dramatically: one sees the three mighty domes of the three religions: the newly restored white dome of the Hurva Synagogue (destroyed in 1948, now resurrected as a defiant Jewish symbol); the golden Dome of the Rock, resplendent and dazzling in the sunlight; and the great dome of the Holy Sepulcher. From the street below one can hear the shrieks of children playing in the schoolyard, the robust hymn-singing of Spanish pilgrims on the Via Dolorosa, and the air-piercing cry of the muezzin and the call to prayer from the minaret; on a Friday at dusk the Jewish siren announcing the arrival of the Sabbath completes the cacophony. Here the traditions face each other. One sister tells me:[5]

> We are all children of God—and children of Abraham! We want to create safe places where genuine encounter can take place. Since the 2000 Intifada [uprising] dialogue has been more difficult—the trust level has deteriorated and the hatred has grown. Fear holds people back. We are teaching Hebrew to our Arabic staff here, because the alternative to demonizing the Other is learning the language of the Other. We have to see the Other as a human being and as a child of God. It would be easy to give up on all this, but we hold on—we have to live the Christian value of hope. We have to stand beside people with hope.

Another Sister speaks of the pain of this street:[6]

> Today the Via Dolorosa is still a way of tears. Here, at the second station Jesus received his cross—and I feel that he still receives it today in the people of the Palestinians, Christian and Muslim. There is a constant cry for help here, and despair all around. They feel that the world is not concerned. They feel unwanted and despised. Jesus continues to suffer in these children. The Via Dolorosa is

5. Sister Trudy (sister of the Convent of Our Lady of Zion, popularly known as the Sisters of Zion Convent), interview with Andrew Mayes in November 2010 at the Sisters of Zion Convent.

6. Sister Rita (sister of the Convent of Our Lady of Zion), interview with Andrew Mayes in November 2010 at the Sisters of Zion Convent.

not just a historical event but a daily reality, and not only on this street but at the checkpoints, where there is daily humiliation and degradation for children just trying to get to school or folk to work. Some of our staff have to queue up each day for two hours and they are treated like animals at the checkpoints. Even here, on this street, sometimes the city gate is closed and we can't get food supplies in for the guesthouse, or building supplies. The frustration level is sometimes very high. There are daily complications with soldiers everywhere and restrictions imposed all the time. But is still a privilege to live here, so close to where Jesus walked. Our role is to walk alongside others on this way of sorrows. As John puts it, "Walk in the same manner" [1 John 2: 6]. He says to us: "I have no hands but yours now." So Palestinians have a heavy cross to bear and we walk with them. But living in the Muslim Quarter and also working with the Jewish people, makes us open to both. We do not take sides—there have been mistakes on both sides. We can love and respect the Jewish people, even if we do not approve of Israeli policies. And we have to remember: even though Jesus was a Man of Sorrows, he was not a miserable, unhappy person! We remember Christ's suffering and death, but we do continue to live and enjoy life! That is the paradox. Our faith is grounded in suffering. We turn to God and have a greater trust in God when there is difficulty and suffering. God is compassionate. And this road: perhaps more prayers are offered here than any place!

Falling and Standing:
Youth on the Via Dolorosa

Station 3, recalling where Jesus collapses the first time under the weight of the cross and through the fatigue of his torture, is marked by a Polish chapel at the junction where the Via Dolorosa meets El Wad Street. He crashes to the ground and lies in the dust, before pulling himself up once again and standing erect. This theme resonates strongly in the stories of the young people who find themselves here today.

The Jewish people were crushed to the earth in the experience of the Holocaust, but now they find themselves standing upright and defiant. This is represented strongly in the soldiers of the Israeli Defense Force. Dressed in green combat uniforms, two teenage Israeli soldiers stand up, defiant and in control, their automatic rifles slung over their shoulders, finger ever on the trigger. Their presence on the Via Dolorosa reminds us of the military forces Jesus faced: soldiers, based in their barracks in the Antonia Fortress, escorted him along the street (Mark1 5:22), and the commander or centurion stood by the cross (Mark 15:39). Today's soldiers, stationed on the corner outside the third station church, maintain a military presence on the busiest stretch of the Via Dolorosa, where Jews rush down to pray at the Western Wall, where Muslims pray at the Al-Aqsa Mosque, and where Christians follow the Way of the Cross. Nineteen-year-old Shmuel explains:[7]

> This is a problem area. We're here to guard Jewish homes in the Muslim quarter. We also keep a look out as Jewish people go down to the Wall. We don't want them attacked. We have to make sure they're safe as they go to pray. You never know what to expect from the terrorists. We have to look out for anything—even Molotov cocktails [gasoline bombs]. You can feel the tension sometimes. It's not good here, it's not fun. The women soldiers are not allowed here—you know the women serve two years in the army and the men three years, but the women are not put in places like this—it is too difficult, anything could happen! We're proud to be here, because we are protecting the Jewish people. We're proud to serve our country. No more questions!

Close by, a balcony extends over the narrow Via Dolorosa, with three large Israeli flags, the Star of David blowing defiantly in the breeze. The building is identified by a sign which says: *Igud Lohamay*: "the Association of the Fighters of the Battle for Jerusalem." A seminary or yeshiva had been founded here by a Polish

7. Shmuel (soldier, Israeli Defense Force), interview with Andrew Mayes March 2011.

rabbi in 1886. The occupants fled from the building during the 1936 Arab riots, but before they left they put a trusted Arab family in charge, who walled up the entrance to the synagogue or study room on the first floor. It was to remain hidden from view until June 1967, when Israeli soldiers, taking charge of the Old City, regained possession of this building. With great joy they unwalled the synagogue, its contents untouched for thirty-one years. Today it is a thriving traditional yeshiva. Hanuch, a student in his twenties, explains:[8]

> We need to be here. It's our land, our city. Since '67, we are back! We don't like this being called the "Muslim Quarter"—for us, it is the renewed Jewish Quarter, because Jews have been living on this street since the nineteenth century. We are witnessing the Redemption of the Land. We are getting ready for the coming of the Messiah. Today we have two hundred students here, from all over Israel, to study the Torah, to get ready.
>
> We feel safe in the building because we have security guards. But we are not allowed to walk down the street to the Kotel [Western Wall] by ourselves in the evening. We need two armed guards, with their guns ready, to accompany us past the Arab homes and shops. It's just too dangerous for us. The Rabbi forbids us going alone. By day the Arabs concentrate on stealing from the tourists. At night they concentrate on us. They will spit at us, or worse! So we have worry living here. But it's the greatest privilege to be close to where the Temple was, and where one day it will be rebuilt!

Seventeen-year-old Doreen works for a Christian guesthouse nearby, helping in the kitchen after school hours.[9]

> For the Christian young people, we can sometimes feel threatened. We are such a small community. I mean, there are billions of Muslims here, but not many Christians.

8. Hanuch (Jewish yeshiva student), interview by Andrew Mayes in October 2010.

9. Doreen (student), interview by Andrew Mayes in November 2010 at Sisters of Zion Convent, on the Via Dolorosa.

We feel in the minority. Sometimes Christians are afraid. But I still like living here. The shopping is close by! And to live where Jesus walked, that is a great privilege. And we have the rich Palestinian culture here—the music with the drums and the oud [mandolin], the traditional Arab dances. This is our country and we feel very proud of it.

Station 7, recalling where Jesus stumbles and falls the second time, is marked by a chapel at the junction of the Via Dolorosa and the busy Khan ez Zeit—which runs the route of the ancient Roman cardo. Alae, who works with young people for what is now called the Palestinian Counseling Center in Jerusalem's Old City:[10]

The Center's been here for eleven years. It is supported by the Latin Patriarchate. Right now we are helping sixty young people from the Old City and East Jerusalem on drugs, mainly in their twenties. Forty percent of them are injecting heroin. About a quarter are Christians—the rest are Muslims.

They have got trapped in a circle. They are under such pressures. There are no jobs for them, few chances to study, overcrowded homes, no sports facilities on the Arab side of the city. And the Wall [Separation Barrier] cuts them off from their wider families. They feel alone. They take drugs to escape all this, then they get into debt, stealing to support the habit, going into petty crime. Then sometimes they get put in jails or detention centers, but often the Israeli police don't seem to bother with them. The soldiers and police are more preoccupied with security issues, watching over the house evictions and demolitions in Silwan. In the West Bank our police really clamp down on the drugs. But here?

Really the young people are swinging between two worlds: going to the new city, with its discos and parties, and belonging to very traditional families in the Old City, where young people are expected to stay in. Really Arab society here is tribal and individual achievement is

10. Alae, (counselor), interview by Andrew Mayes in November 2010 at the Old City Counselling Center, now called the Palestinian Counseling Center.

not always encouraged. It is not like the individualism of the West with its competition between people.

But there are some young people, of course, who want to aim higher, they have creative ideas and want to make something of themselves. At our center we lead a program for youth empowerment: leadership training. We teach creative thinking, getting them to see what they can do—creative things, art things, in the schools and hospitals—designing things. We try to give them their confidence back. They can be useful—they can do good! They might be pushed down, but they can get up again!

Reaching Out:
Women on the Via Dolorosa

On the Via Dolorosa there are three poignant meetings between Jesus and women. Jesus comes face to face with his mother, as she powerlessly looks on at the agony and distress of her son, a son she once cradled at Bethlehem and nurtured in Nazareth. Later Jesus meets a woman to whom tradition has assigned the name Veronica—meaning "true image." As she steps forward to wipe the bloodied face of Jesus, the imprint of his features is left upon the cloth. Soon afterwards, Jesus encounters a group of women in deepest grief, bewailing him loudly. We meet the women of Jerusalem who live in these sacred spots today.

Station 4 is marked by an Armenian Catholic Church built in 1905, its altar crowned by an octagonal cupola so distinctive of Armenian architecture. In the courtyard outside the church stands a memorial to the Armenian holocaust: the memory of the suffering lies deep within the Armenian collective consciousness. On the street, Aneesa, who is in her forties, sits in the gutter where Jesus met his Mother. She is perched on an upturned plastic crate, meters away from the young Israeli soldiers on duty at the corner where the Via Dolorosa meets the busy El Wad Street (Valley Street). She wears the traditional Palestinian ankle-length dress (black, with stunning embroidery in different colors on the chest) while a white scarf covers her hair. She is surrounded by clusters of vegetables and sells sprigs of basil, parsley, and thyme for two shekels a piece, making thirty shekels a day for her family in Bethlehem. She is always reaching out her hand to passersby. Sitting in the dust of the gutter, she somehow maintains a quiet dignity in the midst of it all. She seems resigned to her fate, but is grateful for everything, for little things. She peppers every sentence with *hamdulillah*—"thanks be to God!"[11]

> I have five children—three girls and two boys, thanks be to God. They are aged between two and twelve; the twelve year old really looks after the family, as my husband is very sick. He is fifty. He can't work; he has big heart problems—he is often in the hospital, and the fees are so high I can hardly pay them. I get home to see the children once in two weeks. I have to sleep rough in the Old City every night, wherever I can find a space! I often get cold but, thanks be to God, I have my jumper. In Bethlehem we all live in one room. That is all we have. No telephone, and I don't have a mobile, to stay in touch with the family. We have electricity—thanks be to God— and we have a well for water.
>
> I could be arrested here, as I am from the West Bank and don't have all the papers and permits to sell things. Somehow I get through the Wall. Here the soldiers leave me alone. They are interested in the young men, always stopping them and asking them for their ID.
>
> I have never stopped to think if things could be any different. We say "enshallah" for everything—"if God wills . . ." I expect nothing. We just survive, week to week. I have no options to do anything else. What else can I do? I don't have hope of any change. But we do survive: thanks be to God. I go to the Al-Aqsa Mosque—that is special. God looks after us. Now you make me smile. You are the first person to take notice of me and speak to me in weeks!

Station 6 is celebrated by a Greek Catholic church dedicated to the memory of Saint Veronica and cared for since 1948 by

11. Aneesa (Palestinian mother), interview by Marion Jadon (on behalf of the author) in November 2010 on Al Wad Street in Jerusalem

Charles de Foucauld's order of Little Sisters of Jesus. Sister Rose, a German, has lived here since 1997 and is part of a community today of five sisters here.[12] The story of the sixth station tells how Veronica, stepping out of the crowd, comes forward to wipe the face of Jesus as he passes, carrying his cross. The imprint of his features is left indelibly on the cloth. How does the community identify with Veronica's experience?

> We aim to live a contemplative life in the midst of the city, to be with God and to be with the people. Like Jesus in Nazareth, we work with our hands, we live a simple, poor life. We try to wipe the face of Jesus today, as we see his face in the poor, in the pilgrims, the Muslim residents of this street, in all people. What is very, very important is building up relationships, bit by bit, with all our neighbors. We share in their good moments and bad, in their births, marriages, and deaths. Our motto is, "Notre vocation est être." Our vocation is being, being here, with Jesus, with the people.
>
> My sorrow is that there is no peace, that the Palestinians continue to suffer. And the local Christians—Arab Christians—what is left for them? We were thinking of this recently in the ecumenical prayer group: we meet every week with other Christians to pray about the situation. We saw three options for Palestinian Christians right now. 1. Go, leave, quit. 2. Live in impossible conditions, not having any rights, any peace. 3. Suffer for your faith, be ready to face martyrdom if necessary. Look, Christians made up 20 percent of Jerusalem in 1948, when we first came here. Today in the city we are just about 1 percent of the population. But Jesus is here; he is with the people. And we are just living in the midst of it all, a tiny witness to Christ's love.

Station 8, marked by a cross in the wall, commemorates the moment Jesus speaks to the women of Jerusalem. Here Steph, a young German evangelical woman, runs Saint John's Hospice, a fourteen-bed guesthouse, with her husband. They are members of

12. Sister Rose (Little Sister of Jesus), interview by Andrew Mayes at Convent of the Little Sisters of Jesus in Jerusalem in October 2010.

the lay evangelical community of Christus-Teff, based in Marburg near Frankfurt, and live here alongside young volunteers as part of a community of five. What is it like to live here? Steph exclaims:[13]

> Oh, the noise! The guesthouse straddles the seventh and eighth stations and the main thoroughfare of Khan ez Zeit. We get woken by the Christians praying noisily at 5am on the street below. We get the call of the muezzin blasted at us five times a day, the constant hubbub of the street below. And sometimes you can feel the tension in the air, you can taste it . . .
>
> But we have our chapel—such stillness, such quietness! There I can reflect on what it means to me to live so close to the spot where Jesus speaks to the women of Jerusalem: "weep for yourselves . . ." [Luke 23:28]. This has a vital message for us today. Jesus is honoring women. Today—the Jewish women are stuck in the home, the Muslim women are oppressed by conventions. Jesus speaks to the women of Jerusalem and he empowers them, he tells them to take responsibility for themselves: "Don't weep for me . . ." He says, don't worry about me, think of yourselves, what you can do. You can change the world bit by bit!
>
> Jesus is giving us a choice, like when he says: "If they do this when the wood is green, what will they do when it is dry?" We always ask guests here, are you dry wood or green wood? Dry wood is cut off from the tree, it is out on a limb, independent, separated, not connected to the life-source. The green wood is being part of the living tree, alive in God's life. So we ask: where are you? Which are you?
>
> Jesus is the peacemaker, but Jesus is for people not for states, for countries. The political struggle is not our fight. My husband always says: "If you are for the Jew but not for the Palestinian, you don't have the heart of God. If you are for the Palestinian but not for the Jew,

13. Steph (warden, Lutheran Johanniter Ordens Hospiz [the German Hospice of the Order of St John]), interview by Andrew Mayes in November 2010 at the hospice.

you don't have the heart of God. If you are for all people, then you have the heart of God in you."

Up the street Hala heads the Melia Art and Training Center (now called the Melia Art & Embroidery Center) on behalf of the Arab Orthodox Society for Relief of the Sick. Established in 1990, it empowers and trains women in needlework skills on the West Bank and here in its shop sells the stunning embroidery—dresses, bags, and stoles—made by the Palestinian women, raising vital cash for families living in poverty. Hala is an active member of the Saint James' Arab Orthodox Church: their parish church is the ancient building adjoining the Holy Sepulcher's great belfry, a stone's throw from Calvary. The Orthodox church has two constituencies: Greek hierarchy and Greek pilgrims, and the local Arabs. Hala testifies:[14]

> Jesus understands the pain of this street. His sufferings, his sacrifice . . . he understands. I ask Jesus to carry what I am carrying, the worry and the stress. This makes me feel more free. He helps me. He says to me: "As I carry the cross for you, bear your burdens patiently. I will carry them with you." So I say to him: "This worry is yours, it's not mine!"
>
> My heart opened to God when I joined with other Christians to pray for justice and for Christian unity in this city. Before, I did follow religion, but it was cold and dutiful. My faith came alive when I joined the ecumenical prayer group—we meet each Tuesday afternoon to encourage each other and to pray for the city. Now I see the resurrection in everything, even in little things—especially in little things: the flower opening on my terrace, the bird dancing in the sunlight. These are precious gifts of God. These are signs of spiritual life. You see the resurrection every day in your life, and in the strength you get. We live the resurrection in everything. His rising is everyday. And I always hope that tomorrow will be better than today! Jesus gives us love to share with the Muslims,

14. Hala Jahshan (manager of Melia Art Center—now called the Melia Art & Embroidery Center), interview by Andrew Mayes December 2010 at the Center

and with those who are difficult to love. We have to care for our neighbors and for the weak. His rising is everyday. Look for it!

Bearing Burdens:
Men on the Via Dolorosa

Station 5, recalling how Simon of Cyrene helps Jesus carry his cross, is marked by a small chapel on the corner of El Wad street. The Gospel of Mark tells us three things about Simon (15:21). First, he was from Cyrene, in North Africa: he represents the outsider, the immigrant, reflecting Jerusalem's vocation to be a universal city, for all humanity. This is reinforced, second, by the reference to Simon "coming in from the country": perhaps he was a laborer, a workman coming into the city to find employment. Third, we learn that he was a father (his children's names are given to us): he carries all the responsibilities and worries of a parent. He gets caught up in the drama and finds the crossbeam placed on his shoulders. At this very point today in the street, we encounter a range of men, each in his own way carrying a heavy burden, some feeling they are outsiders in this city: all are sons or fathers with anxieties for their future. Some, like Jesus, feel crushed into the ground by the cross they have to bear.

Nearby twenty-eight-year-old Haitham helps run a shop selling ancient Russian icons. Steps lead off the shop into a cave with shelves stacked from floor to ceiling with ancient pots, plates, vessels of all kinds. Haitham beams.[15]

> Welcome to Ali Baba's cave! Look at this oil lamp. It is from Herod's time, Jesus' time. Now we are about three meters down. This is the true street level of the Via Dolorosa! You know, our family is mentioned in the Qur'an. When the prophet Mohammed—peace be upon him—went from Mecca to Medina, our family welcomed him, we were his protectors and companions and

15. Haitham (Arab shopkeeper), interview by Andrew Mayes in December 2010.

he stayed with us. Our noble family came to Jerusalem fourteen hundred years ago. We hold the keys of the Al-Aqsa Mosque! Things are so different in Jerusalem. You know, when we travel away, it is always a joy to come back here. It is holy—holy for all, Muslim, Christian, Jew. You feel different here, special. Even the food tastes different! It is one thing when my mother cooks outside the city, and another when she cooks here. She uses the same ingredients, but here it tastes so different! Sure, the conflict makes things difficult for us, but somehow I feel safe here. It is my home.

Tucked away behind the façades of shops which line the Via Dolorosa near the fifth station are found very different workshops. Fifty-year-old Daoud has a small house adjoining both the station's chapel and a synagogue owned by the Institute of Talmudic Studies, established in a building taken over in 1999. Daoud had stones thrown at his children playing in the courtyard below when the Old City settlers first moved in above the synagogue, but it is calmer now. He runs a small workshop here and is an accomplished craftsman in olive wood, fashioning figures of Jesus carrying his cross for pilgrims.[16]

I love this wood. The olive tree is very special to us Palestinians. Its roots go deep down into the soil, like us. It belongs to the land. It is us and our future. The trees give us oil, for soap and cooking and medicine, and wood for this carving. It makes me so angry when I hear that settlers cut down thousands of our trees this year, and the Wall has destroyed so many. This wood—look at it—the clear parts and the parts with such lovely grain. When the wood is green it can be cut quickly by machine, but I work with the dry wood and do it all by hand. I choose each piece carefully. It takes me three days to make each piece. I cannot sell it for ten shekels! It is my life! We cut the wood carefully so it doesn't hurt the tree. We may take off a branch but you know, the olive tree never dies. It will grow again another branch. Like us!

16. Daoud (Arab shopkeeper), interview by Andrew Mayes December 2010.

The pilgrims on the street don't often stop to buy anything from my shop here. They keep their heads down in their prayerbooks and beads—they are so caught up in their prayers they don't seem even to notice us. They don't stop to speak to us! Christians need to open their eyes!

Another workshop is hidden away. Across the street, a narrow passage contains an assortment of brooms and brushes for sale. Nadira, in her thirties, oversees a workshop beneath ancient vaults, where nine blind men, between ages twenty and sixty, silently and skillfully make brooms, feeling with trained fingertips what needs to be done. They all wear darkened glasses—perhaps to cover an eye deformity or to shield their delicate eyes from bright sunlight.[17]

The Arab Association for the Blind was founded in the time of the British Mandate, in 1932. We teach basic skills to the blind, so they can make a living or just survive. Our little shop sells the brooms to raise some money for their families—they are all very poor. The men come from Bethlehem or Ramallah. Somehow they get through the checkpoint at the Wall each day. But some don't make it; they are turned back. So some men, and women too, make the brooms in their own homes—we get the raw materials to them. They can sell things in their local markets. They are not all old—look, some of these are young men. We help about a hundred and fifty blind people altogether, here, in Hebron, and in Amman. We are trying to get funds to found a Braille printing house. We want them to read. We want to give them a chance.

Station 9, where Jesus falls the third time, is marked by an ancient pillar outside the Coptic Church of Saint Helena. Here sits

17. Nadira Bazbaz (director of the Arab Association for the Blind), interview by Andrew Mayes in December 2010 at her workshop on the Via Dolorosa.

Father Mikael, a Coptic priest for forty-three years. He has lived here for eleven years.[18]

> I love it here. Fourteen monks live here. We welcome pilgrims every day to the Coptic church and this great cistern which Helena built. But sometimes I miss the great silence of my monastery of Anba Bishoi in the Wadi Natrun of Egypt. It goes back to the fourth century, it is a monastery of the desert fathers. Here is it very noisy. But I am very happy to live here.
>
> My biggest pain is for the Christians of Egypt. The Muslims are against us. In Cairo they burn pictures of our Coptic pope after Friday prayers. They spit at it and abuse it. They take our women. They give us Christians no jobs. They are against us. We are pushed down all the time, like Jesus at the ninth station. We are pushed down, down, down.

Dying and Rising:
Pastors on the Via Dolorosa

Station 10, where Jesus is stripped prior to his crucifixion, is to be found in the awesome Basilica of the Holy Sepulcher, in the Latin chapel beside Calvary. It can be reached by crossing the Ethiopian monastery, a community stripped of its rights but dignified in its faith. This is an African village in the heart of Jerusalem. On the roof of Saint Helena's Chapel—that part of the Holy Sepulcher exposing the deep quarry where Constantine's mother found the true Cross—lives a community of five Ethiopian monks. Their little monastic cells have been built of mud bricks amid the ruins of the medieval Crusader cloister, but the Ethiopian Christian presence in Jerusalem goes back to at least the fourth century. Gerama, in his seventies, who has lived nearby since 1968, helps look after the property and is involved in the pastoral care of the community. He speaks of the two proudest Ethiopian traditions linked to the

18. Fr. Mikael (Coptic priest), interview by Andrew Mayes in November 2010, in Church of Saint Helena in Jerusalem.

Bible. Looking up to the sky, raising his arms in a gesture towards heaven, Gerama exclaims:[19]

> This is the Monastery of the King, we call it "Deir es Sultan." The Bible tells you about the visit of our queen, the queen of Sheba, to King Solomon, son of David. Solomon fathered with her the first emperor of Ethiopia, Menelik. And the Acts of the Apostles tells you about the conversion of the first Ethiopian by Saint Philip as he traveled the road from Jerusalem to Gaza. He is the first Ethiopian Christian. So we have been coming here ever since!
>
> We have only five sisters here now up the street in the convent and they are very old. And we have five brothers living here on the roof. They rise for prayers at four every morning. They cook for themselves very simple stuff; they are very poor. I see tears in their eyes very often . . . My joy? I have one joy, despite it all. Living here is the gift of God!

Station 11, commemorating the nailing of Jesus, and station 12, commemorating the death of Jesus, are marked by chapels built atop the rocky limestone outcrop of Calvary, and nearby the tomb of Jesus recalls stations 13 and 14, recalling the taking down of Jesus' body from the cross, and the burial. A stone's throw away stands the Lutheran Church of the Redeemer, where Ibrahim Azar has been pastor to a congregation of four hundred, drawn from members from ninety families. In 2017 he was elected bishop for the Evangelical Lutheran Church in Jordan and the Holy Land. The church's four schools educate Christian and Muslim students side by side and have a strong ethos of teaching tolerance and peacebuilding.[20]

> We all identify with Jesus in the cross. He identifies with us. Our Christian young people are so isolated and vulnerable. They are cut from their brothers and sisters

19. Gerama (Ethiopian monk), interview by Andrew Mayes in October 2010 at Ethiopian monastery.

20. Ibrahim Azar (Arabic pastor of the Lutheran Church of the Redeemer), interview by Andrew Mayes in December 2010 at his church.

in the West Bank. We used to do so much together, but now the West Bank youth can't come to Jerusalem—they don't get permits. Our own young people in the Old City feel alone, separated. There are such a few of them—we have only twenty in our own youth group. How will they find partners? Christians are so few in the Old City, and they cannot marry Muslims or Jews. They can't make relationships with their peers on the West Bank as they used to do. I fear for the future of Christians in the Holy City. This is our city and our land, but we are leaving all the time. The young people are our future—but what future is that?

What we have to remember is this: God didn't stay on the cross. He didn't stay in the tomb. He went out and gave life to the people. We live now between Easter and the great resurrection at the end. We have to place our present troubles in this big perspective, and not let them cloud our hope. We are people of faith. We live in the faith of the resurrection!

Questions for Reflection

Reflecting on your encounters with each group, consider these three questions and look up the pertinent scriptures:

1. What does this say to you in your situation?

2. What lines in the scriptures and interviews strike you? Why?

3. What are the sorrows and hopes of this age range or group in your own neighborhood? How can you and friends respond to them?

Children: Read Mark 9:31–37; 10:13–16 (child in the midst).

Youth: Read 1 John 1:12–17 (an address to young men).

Women: Read Luke 23:27–31 (Jesus speaks to the women).

Men: Read 2 Timothy 1:3–7 (Paul's advice to Timothy)

Pastors: Read Romans 6: 1–14 (Easter hope).

Prayer Exercise

Today's Way of the Cross

The petitions are grouped in threes, and one phrase of "Lord have mercy, Christ have mercy, Lord have mercy" may be said after each. At each station, the first two petitions relate to Jerusalem today, and the third relates to our own home situation.

Jesus is condemned to death

Jesus, you are judged before Pilate: give the little ones of this street a carefree childhood, free from the oppressive judgment or control of others.

Jesus, you are crowned with thorns: heal the trauma of all children damaged by the violence of others.

Jesus, scourged and beaten, enable us to draw close to those who are bruised in our own communities.

Jesus receives his cross

Jesus, the cross is laid upon your shoulders: give to parents wisdom and patience as they accept the weight of their responsibilities in an uncertain world.

Jesus, you begin your journey: bless the Sisters of Zion and inspire all the children of Abraham—Jews, Muslims, and Christians—to walk the risky journey of mutual understanding and trust.

Jesus, Man of Sorrows and Man of Joy, help us to restore laughter to children who are robbed of childhood innocence.

Jesus falls first time

Jesus, you are crushed with the weight of the cross: give to Shmuel and all soldiers compassion and humanity in their dealings with others.

Jesus, you find yourself in the dust of the street, give to Hanuch and to all the students of the Jewish yeshiva the grace to study your Law in humility and tolerance.

Jesus, you are brought low: lead us from sympathy to empathy, and give us the grace to get right alongside the brokenhearted and downcast.

Jesus meets his mother

Jesus, you receive Mary's touch: comfort all parents anxious for the fate of the children.

Jesus, you are sustained by Mary's look into your eyes: restore dignity to Aneesa and all who find themselves in the gutter of the street.

Jesus, your heart goes out to your own mother: give us the wisdom to speak words of encouragement to all mothers who are stressed or depressed.

Simon of Cyrene helps carry the cross

Jesus, you need Simon's help in bearing the cross: sustain Haitham, Daoud, and the men of the city who carry heavy weight of fear and insecurity and worry for their families.

Jesus, you share our infirmities: cheer and hearten Nadira and the blind men of this street.

Jesus, you accepted the support of another: help us to step out from the crowd to relieve the burdens of those hurting in our community.

Veronica wipes the face of Jesus

Jesus, you accept Veronica's gesture of comfort: bless the Little Sisters of Jesus as they extend Veronica's loving touch today.

Jesus, you reveal your face to Veronica: help us to discern your features in the lives of those who suffer.

Jesus, you give an imprint to Veronica's cloth: impress on our hearts the image of your love.

Jesus falls the second time

Jesus, you are crushed by the weight of the cross: lighten the hearts of all young people burdened by frustration and loss of opportunity.

Jesus, you find yourself brought low once again: raise up to a new future young people pulled down by drug abuse and loss of self-worth.

Jesus, falling down and rising again, give us courage, vision, and perseverance to develop our ministry among young people where we live.

Jesus meets the women of Jerusalem

Jesus, you greet the women of the city: hearten and empower Jewish, Muslim, and Christian women, who seek to take new responsibility for their futures, as we remember Aneesa, Sister Rose, Steph, and Hala.

Jesus, you look upon the tears of the women: strengthen all women who are degraded, exploited, or oppressed.

Jesus, you honored the potential of the women of Jerusalem: show us how to welcome and respect the dignity and gifting of women in our churches today.

Jesus falls the third time

Jesus, you stumble again to the ground: sustain and uplift the most fragile and vulnerable Christians of Jerusalem; we remember Gerama and Father Mikael.

Jesus, your body is fatigued and broken: heal the wounds in your body the church.

Jesus, torn and bruised of body, help us to work for the unity of your people in our locality.

Jesus is stripped

Jesus, you are stripped of your clothes: restore the dignity of all who feel denuded and exposed to danger.

Jesus, you are exposed to abuse: we pray for those who hurl insults at one another in this city today.

Jesus, bearing our shame, strip us of all judgmental attitudes and hardness of heart.

Jesus is nailed to the cross

Jesus, you open wide your arms to embrace the world: encompass with your love all who are seeking the Divine today across the globe.

Jesus, your body is pierced with five wounds: draw close to those wounded by violent actions in the city of Jerusalem.

Jesus, help us to leave at the cross our failures, our fears and our frustrations.

Jesus dies on the cross

Jesus, dying on the cross, help Ibrahim and all pastors to reflect your undying love to others.

Jesus, you share utterly and completely the pains of humanity: enfold and embrace those who suffer in the Holy Land today.

Jesus, breathing your last, help us to exhale from our hearts every judgmental attitude towards others.

The body of Jesus is taken down from the cross

Jesus, laid in the arms of your mother, comfort all who grieve for losses or bereavements of any kind.

Jesus, your life looks finished and over: draw close to those trapped in despondency or fatalism.

Jesus, you are the new Adam opening up a new future for the world: fill with unshakable hope all who work for peace and reconciliation.

The body of Jesus is laid in the tomb

Jesus, your body is safely placed in the tomb: bless all who care for and protect the holy places today.

Jesus, awaiting resurrection, be close to all Jews, Christians, and Muslims who find themselves watching and waiting for a better world.

Jesus, in the deepest darkness you kindle the light of new life: ignite and enflame in us the faith of Easter, that with the Christians of Jerusalem we may witness to your gospel by lives radiant and incandescent with your glory, Amen!

Further Reading

Armstrong, Karen. *Jerusalem: One City, Three Faiths.* New York: Knopf, 1996.

Ateek, Naim Stifan. *Contemporary Way of the Cross.* Jerusalem: Sabeel Ecumenical Liberation Center, 2005.

———. *A Palestinian Christian Cry for Reconciliation.* Maryknoll, NY: Orbis, 2008.

Ellis, Marc H. *Revolutionary Forgiveness: Essays on Judaism, Christianity, and the Future of Religious Life.* Waco: Baylor University Press, 2000.

Qleibo, Ali Hussein. *Jerusalem in the Heart.* Jerusalem: Kloreus, 2000.

FIGURE 7

7

Through the Damascus Gate

Sharing Pathways to the Divine

"I KISS THE WALLS at the Damascus Gate every time I get back to Jerusalem. This is one of the wonders of the world! The sights, the smells, but most of all the holy places invigorate me."[1]

Twenty-two-year-old Abed works on Jerusalem's Via Dolorosa at his dad's shop, and studies business part-time at the Arab American University at Jenin. His excitement announces to us that the Damascus Gate ushers us into another world, and plunges us into the sights, sounds, and smells of the Holy City from the north side. From the road flights of steps lead the pilgrim down to the greatest of Jerusalem's portals, flanked by two towers with stunning crenellations, built by Suleiman the Magnificent in the sixteenth century. The gate takes its name from the Syrian capital, 135 miles away, to which a historic road led: Paul's road to Damascus. Jewish people call it Sha'ar Shkhem because this road also leads to ancient Shechem. The Arabic name, Bab al-Amud, Gate of the Column, recalls that at this very spot Hadrian built a triple-arched gate with a freestanding column when he remodeled Jerusalem as the Roman city he called Aelia Capitolina.

---

1. Abed (student), interview by Andrew Mayes in November 2010 at his father's shop on the Via Dolorosa.

The Damascus Gate is shared by Jewish, Muslim, and Christian pilgrims who find themselves walking side by side down towards their respective holy places. Sometimes it looks as if they exist in parallel universes: rabbis keeping their eyes on their open prayer book and reciting psalms as they make their passage; Christian pilgrims ambling down, intent to reach the Church of the Resurrection without giving in to the temptations of the bazaar with its colorful and enticing wares and sweets. But there is always a sense of normally good-natured jostling—physical contact between the traditions is unavoidable amid the pressing throngs.[2] The Damascus Gate, then, invites us to name and celebrate common themes across the traditions we have encountered—commonalities, shared themes, and experiences of the Divine that illuminate each other. In particular we identify four paradoxes that each tradition experiences and wrestles with—recalling that a paradox is a mystery to be lived, not a problem to be solved!

Naming the Unnameable

A recurrent theme in various traditions is devotion to the divine names. Jacob's question sums up the quest:

> Then Jacob asked him, "Please tell me your name." But he said, "Why is it that you ask my name?" And there he blessed him. So Jacob called the place Peniel, saying, "For I have seen God face to face, and yet my life is preserved." (Gen 32:29,30).

This enigmatic passage in Genesis, in which Jacob struggles with an angel or a man in the waters of the Jabbok River, expresses the paradox at the heart of Judaism regarding the naming of God. Jacob desires to learn the name of the divine combatant but is

2. A courageous dialogue between faiths, involving patient listening to deepen mutual understanding, takes place in Jerusalem, exemplified by the interfaith work of Jerusalem Peacebuilders, Inter-Religious Coordinating Council in Israel, the Jerusalem Center for Interreligious Encounter, the Ecumenical Theological Research Fraternity in Israel, and the Sisters of Zion in the Via Dolorosa.

denied his request. He senses he has struggled with the Divine, but he does not come close to discovering the divine name or identity. When Moses later encounters God in the burning bush, he asks God:

> "If I come to the Israelites and say to them, 'The God of your ancestors has sent me to you,' and they ask me, 'What is his name?' what shall I say to them?" God said to Moses, "I am who I am . . . say to the Israelites, 'I am has sent me to you.'" God also said to Moses, "Thus you shall say to the Israelites, 'The Lord, the God of your ancestors, the God of Abraham, the God of Isaac, and the God of Jacob, has sent me to you: This is my name forever, and this my title for all generations'" (Exod 3:13–15).

What is given to Moses here is the Tetragrammaton (lit. "word of four letters")—the four letters representing the divine name YHWH (rendered by Christians, adding the vowels to these consonants, as Yahweh or Jehovah). These letters derive from the Hebrew verb *hayah,* "to be," and can be translated "I am what I am" or "I will be what I will be." Later, on Sinai Moses is given a commandment that says, "You shall not make wrongful use of the name of the LORD your God" (Exod 20:7). This leads later Jewish tradition to avoid all use of the name of the Deity and even when writing it to put "G-d." Does this not contradict the divine command to people to "make known his name" (Isa 12:4; Ps 105:1) and "sing praises to his name" (Ps 68:4)? Rabbis explain that the divine name can be used in worship and prayer with reverence and awe but not in common speech where there may be a blasphemy or dishonor. But the paradox remains, for in Kabbalah there is devotion to the names of God. Rabbi Gikatilla (1248–1310) explains, for example, that one should use the names in prayer according to the divine virtue sought or needed at that particular moment: "One should be aware that all the names mentioned in the Torah are the keys for anything a person needs in the world."[3] Hence the Tree of Life celebrating the *sefirot* can be understood as a meditation on the names of God in this manner:

3. Gikatilla, *Gates of Light=Sha'arei Orah,* introduction.

Creator: Eheieh (I Am)
Understanding: Yahweh Elohim (LORD GOD)   **Wisdom:** Yahweh (LORD)
Intention: Eloh (Almighty)   **Compassion:** El (Mighty One)
Creativity: Eloah Va-Daath (God Manifest)
Observation: Elohim Sabaoth   **Eternity:** Yahweh Sabaoth
(GOD/LORD of Hosts)
Manifesting: El Chai (Mighty Living One)
Healing: Adonai he-Aretz (Lord of Earth)

The founder of Hasidism and a pioneer of Kabbalah, Israel ben Eliezer (1698–1760), was called "Good Master of the Name" (Baal Shem Tov). From the outset, Kabbalah has had deepest devotion to the unspeakable Tetragrammaton and the *sefirot,* which we can articulate and welcome into our lives.

Regarding the Hebrew Scriptures, Kallistos Ware explains,

> In the Hebrew tradition, to do a thing in the name of another, or to invoke and call upon his name, are acts of weight and potency. To invoke a person's name is to make that person effectively present . . . The power and glory of God are present and active in his Name . . . attentively and deliberately to invoke God's Name is to place oneself in his presence, to open oneself to his energy, to offer oneself as an instrument and a living sacrifice in his hands.[4]

This is taken into Orthodox spirituality through the use of the Jesus prayer, where the name of Jesus is repeated on every knot of the Orthodox prayer rope. In an interesting parallel with the Sufi practice of *dhikr*, whereby the remembrance of God is sustained by recital of the name Allah, Christian Orthodox spirituality often links the practice of the remembrance of God with the repetition of the Savior's name. Russian mystic Saint Theophan the Recluse (1815–1894) wrote:

> The recollection (or remembrance) of God is mentally standing before God in the heart.

4. Ware, *Power of the Name*, 12.

Everywhere and always God is with us, near to us and in us. But we are not always with Him, since we do not remember Him; and because we do not remember Him, we allow ourselves many things which we would not permit if we did remember. The more firmly you are established in the recollection of God, the more quiet your thoughts will become and the less they will wander.

Remembrance of God is something that God Himself grafts upon the soul. But the soul must force itself to persevere and to toil. Work, making every effort to attain the unceasing remembrance of God, and God, seeing how fervently you desire it will give you this constant remembrance of Himself.

To succeed in this remembrance it is advisable to accustom oneself to the continual repetition of the Jesus Prayer, "Lord Jesus Christ, Son of God, have mercy on me," holding in mind the thought of God's nearness, His presence in the heart.[5]

Christian spirituality celebrates two contrasting but complementary approaches to the Divine. The *kataphatic* tradition of prayer permits affirmations and declarations about God to be made confidently: we believe that the Divine has revealed itself to humanity. But we realize that words fail: in the *apophatic* tradition, words give way to silence, concepts about God dissolve into speechless wonder. Certainly the kataphatic tradition, the *via positiva*, which delights in vivid metaphors and images, needs to be complemented by the apophatic way, the *via negativa*, which tells us that we need to go beyond images, or attempts at naming the Divine—they are only a starting point. Meister Eckhart affirmed: "the freer you are from images the more receptive you are to his interior operation."[6] Writing of the unknowability of God, Orthodox theologian Danielou puts it,

5. Quoted in a 2004 talk by Mother Dorothea, "Discerning and Doing God's Will by Remembering Him in a World of Distraction," at Saint Andrew the Fool-for-Christ Serbian Orthodox Church (http://orthodoxinfo.com/praxis/rememberinggod.aspx/).

6. Quoted in Fleming, ed., *Meister Eckhart*, 90.

After learning all that can be known of God, the soul discovers the limits of this knowledge; and this discovery is an advance, because now there is an awareness of the divine transcendence and incomprehensibility. We have then arrived at a negative, "apophatic" theology. For we have now an authentic experience, a true vision. And the darkness is a positive reality that helps us to know God—that is why it is called luminous. For it implies an awareness of God that transcends all determination, and thus it is far truer than any determined categorical knowledge. For here in this obscurity the soul experiences the transcendence of the divine nature, that infinite distance by which God surpasses all creation.[7]

Rowan Williams in his classic *The Wound of Knowledge* reminds us, writing of John of the Cross:

Illumination is the running-out of language and thought, the compulsion exercised by a reality drastically and totally beyond the reach of our conceptual apparatus . . . Real knowledge of God cannot be put into words with any approximation to completeness; thus real and personal knowledge of God cannot be identified with words in the understanding . . . God himself breaks and reshapes all religious language as he acts through vulnerability, failure and contradiction.[8]

The Islamic tradition's devotion to the ninety-nine names of God derives from a saying or hadith of Muhammad: "Truly there are ninety-nine names of God, one hundred minus one. He who enumerates and believes in them and the one God behind them would get into Paradise." Some Muslims use a rosary (*Tasbih*), in order to recite the ninety-nine names. In Islam, the hundredth name of God is unpronounceable and unknown to humans. The

7. Danielou, "Introduction" in Musurillo, trans. and ed., *From Glory to Glory*, 30. Gregory also develops this in reference to his interpretation of the Song of Songs where the divine darkness is characterized not only by unknowing but also by desire and yearning on the part of the bride.

8. Williams, *Wound of Knowledge*, 172, 173, 180. Classic examples of the Christian apophatic way include Gregory of Nyssa's *Life of Moses* and the fourteenth century English text *The Cloud of Unknowing*.

first two names are used in the well-known formula "In the name of God, Most Gracious, Most Merciful," which prefaces every verse in the Qur'an.[9]

> Most Gracious, Most Merciful, King, Holy, Peace, Guarantor, Guardian, Preserver, Almighty, Irresistible, Tremendous, Creator, Rightful, Fashioner of Forms, Forgiving, All Compelling, Bestower, Providing, Opener, All Knowing, Restrainer, Expander, Abaser, Exalter, Giver of Honor, Giver of Dishonor, All Hearing, All Seeing, Judge, Just, Kind, All Aware, Forbearing, Magnificent, All Forgiving, Grateful, Exalted, Great, Preserver, Nourisher. Reckoner. Majestic, Bountiful, Watchful, Responsive, All Encompassing, Wise, Loving, Kind One. Glorious, Raiser of The Dead, Witness, Real, Dependable, Strong, Firm, Steadfast, Protecting Friend, All Praiseworthy, Accounter, Numberer of All, Originator, and Initiator of All, The Reinstater Who Brings Back All, Giver of Life, Bringer of Death, Ever Living, Sustainer of All, Finder, Illustrious, Unique, All Inclusive, Impregnable, All Able, All Determiner, He Who Brings Forward, He Who Puts Far Away, First, Last, Manifest, Hidden, All Encompassing, Exalted, Ever Relenting, Avenger, Pardoner, Compassionate, All Sovereign, Lord of Majesty and Generosity, Requiter, Unifier, All Rich, Enricher, Emancipator, Shielder, Benefactor, Light, Guide, Incomparable, Enduring, Inheritor of All, Guide, Infallible Teacher and Knower, Patient, The Timeless.

We recall that Sheikh Ahram told us: *"As we recite God's Name, we are reborn in the road to Allah. Our hearts become full of mercy, love and giving."* What is happening as one recites the divine names?

---

9. There are variations in lists. The following derives from https://www.pro-quo.com/99-names-of-god-islam.html/. Each Name should be prefaced by the definite article, *the*.

Divinization within Mortality

In many traditions, the divine attributes celebrated in these ways become internalized, appropriated, in the worshiper: what was "out there" comes "in here"; what is an objective truth in the Deity becomes a subjective experience in the human. Through the recital of the divine names, mystical transformation takes place. Orthodox Christians committed to the recital of the name of the Savior through the frequent use of the Jesus Prayer express this in terms of divinization, deification, *theosis:* becoming divine or godlike. This resonates with the New Testament concept of *metamorphosis.* Paul emphasizes our call to be transformed into Christ: "Do not be conformed to this world, but be transformed by the renewing of your minds" (Rom 12:2). In another place he puts it this way: "And all of us, with unveiled faces, seeing the glory of the Lord as though reflected in a mirror, are being transformed into the same image from one degree of glory to another; for this comes from the Lord, the Spirit (2 Cor 3:18). The Greek word Paul uses, *metamorphosis,* denotes a process of profound change. The key transformation is growth into Christ-likeness, closer resemblance to Christ, increasing identification with Christ, fulfilling the promise of baptism. As John puts it, "We can be sure that we are in God only when the one who claims to be living in him is living the same kind of life Christ lived . . . we will be like him because we will see him as he is" (1 John 2:6, 3:2, JB).

In the fourth century Basil the Great affirmed in his treatise *On the Holy Spirit:* "What is set before us is, so far as is possible with human nature, to be made like unto God."[10] Teaching that the Holy Spirit in prayer forms human beings in virtue, Basil expresses a major concern that monastic and Christian training pursue *eusebia*—"a life pleasing to God," characterized by compassion and prayer. As Ellen Charry puts it, "Unless educated to grasp God's majesty and grace, we should fail to understand God properly and be moved to virtuous living as a consequence."[11] Maximus the

10. Basil, *On the Holy Spirit* 1:1.

11. Charry, *By the Renewing of Your Minds,* 115.

Confessor, "father of Byzantine theology," taught in the seventh century:

> The intellect [mind] is granted the grace of theology when, carried on wings of love it is taken up into God and with the help of the Holy Spirit discerns—as far as this is possible for the human intellect—the qualities of God . . .[T]ry to discern, as far as possible, the qualities that appertain to His nature—qualities of eternity, infinity, . . goodness, wisdom and the power of creating, preserving and judging creatures, and so on. For he who discovers these qualities, to however small an extent, is a great theologian.[12]
>
> . . .
>
> The intellect joined to God for long periods through prayer and love becomes wise, good, powerful, compassionate, merciful and long-suffering; in short, it includes within itself almost all the divine qualities. But when the intellect withdraws from God and attaches itself to material things, either it becomes self-indulgent like some domestic animal, or like a wild beast it fights with men for the sake of these things.[13]

Vladimir Lossky explains:

> We must live the dogma expressing a revealed truth, which appears to us as an unfathomable mystery, in such a fashion that instead of assimilating the mystery to our mode of understanding, we should, on the contrary, look for a profound change, an inner transformation of spirit, enabling us to experience it mystically. Far from being mutually opposed, theology and mysticism support and complete each other. One is impossible without the other.[14]

For Lossky, mysticism is defined as "acquired experience of the mysteries of the faith."[15] Orthodoxy views prayer as transformative.

---

12 Maximus the Confessor, in Palmer et al., trans., *Philokalia*, 2:69.

13. Maximus the Confessor, in Palmer et al., trans., *Philokalia*, 2:74.

14. Lossky, *Mystical Theology*, 8.

15. Lossky, *Mystical Theology*, 236.

We recall Lossky's conviction: "To see the divine light . . . as the disciples saw it on Mount Tabor, we must participate in and be transformed by it, according to our capacity. Mystical experience implies this change in our nature, its transformation by grace." This entails "forgetfulness of self, the full flowering of personal consciousness in grace."[16]

Representing Islamic mysticism, Sheikh Ahram speaks of an internalization and assimilation into one's being of the divine attributes: *"The divine names we recite become part of us, they get inside of us. The key feeling, as I said, is to love God and to be filled with love, and to carry this into our daily life."*[17]

But the paradox remains. Baba Farid had spoken often of both our capacity for the Divine and our mortality; of both our destiny for dust and our possibility for transcendence. He frequently repeated these words:

> I pray to live only for the sake of loving Thee,
>
> I wish to become dust and dwell eternally under Thy feet.
>
> My principal expectation from both worlds is that
>
> I should die and live for Thee.[18]

In his own unselfconscious way, Francis of Assisi delights in the attributes of God, seeking "a sense of the Divine" and praying that divine attributes become part of humble living. Scholars[19] believe that his encounter in 1219 with the sultan of Egypt, as we noted above, led Francis to compose this prayer of praise on Mount La Verna in September 1224, when he received the stigmata:

> You are holy Lord God Who does wonderful things.
> You are strong. You are great. You are the most high.
> You are the almighty king. You holy Father,
> King of heaven and earth.
> You are three and one, the Lord God of gods;

16. Lossky, *Mystical Theology*, 224, 231.

17. Sheikh Mazen Ahram. (inspector of the Al-Aqsa Mosque), interview by Andrew Mayes June 2014 at St George's College in Jerusalem.

18. Baba Farid in Qalandar, *Khayr al-majalis*, 224.

19. See, for example, Moses, *Saint and the Sultan*.

> You are the good, all good, the highest good,
> Lord God living and true.
> You are love, charity; You are wisdom, You are humility,
> You are patience, You are beauty, You are meekness,
> You are security, You are rest,
> You are gladness and joy, You are our hope, You are justice,
> You are moderation, You are all our riches to sufficiency.
> You are beauty, You are meekness,
> You are the protector, You are our custodian and defender,
> You are strength, You are refreshment. You are our hope,
> You are our faith, You are our charity,
> You are all our sweetness, You are our eternal life:
> Great and wonderful Lord, Almighty God, Merciful Savior.[20]

Strongly reflecting Islamic devotion to the divine names, this Christian liturgy reminds us that deep learning and deepened prayer can come from an attentive listening to another's spiritual tradition.

Body and Soul / Heart and Mind

It is significant that Francis composed this prayer while experiencing profound physical and bodily changes, receiving the marks of the passion in his hands, feet, and side. A recurring theme we have encountered elsewhere in this book concerns the use of the body in prayer. What do you recall from the different traditions we have observed in Jerusalem? Before you read further, call to mind what physical practices we've met in relation to the practice of prayer . . .

- Jewish *davening*, rhythmic rocking motions of the body
- Sufi dancing and swaying and movement of the head
- Orthodox breathing in and out the Jesus Prayer
- Franciscan walking in processions, including the Way of the Cross, and praying cross prayers with outstretched arms.
- Syriac prostrations in Lent

20. Armstrong et al., eds., *Francis of Assisi*, 1:109.

How can we understand the relationship between physicality and spirituality, between body and soul? What is the mutual interaction? A point of intersection is the heart—at once a physical organ central to human health and the symbolic center of the spiritual person. *The Catechism of the Catholic Church* reminds us that "according to Scripture, it is the *heart* that prays . . . The heart is the dwelling-place where I am, where I live; according to the Semitic or biblical expression, the heart is the place 'to which I withdraw.' The heart is our hidden center . . . the place of encounter, because as image of God we live in relation."[21] Pope Benedict XVI puts it this way: "In Biblical language, the Heart (*Leb*) indicates the center of human life, the point where reason, will, temperament and sensitivity converge, where the person finds his unity and his interior orientation."[22] According to the Hebraic tradition, the heart is the center of the human, uniting the intellectual, emotional, and volitional functions of the person.[23] It stands as a potent symbol of the inner life that is embodied and incarnate.

The heart image enables a dialogue between Eastern and Western perspectives on prayer. Ware reminds us that in Orthodox theology "the heart signifies the deep self; it is the seat of wisdom and understanding, the place where our moral decisions are made, the inner shrine in which we experience divine grace and the indwelling of the Holy Trinity. It indicates the human person as a 'spiritual subject,' created in God's image and likeness."[24] Ware goes on: "Here is no head-heart dichotomy, for the intellect is *within* the heart. The heart is the meeting point between body and soul, between the subconscious, conscious and supraconscious, between the human and the divine."[25] Abbot Ephraim reminds us: "St John Damascene remarks that 'as the eyes are to the body, so the intellect is to the soul' . . . this function of the intellect is an

21. Catholic Church, *Catechism*, 545 (italics original).

22. Quoted in Church Union, *Order*, 39.

23. See Wolff, *Anthropology*.

24. Ware, *Inner Kingdom*, 62.

25. Ware, "Ways of Prayer and Contemplation I: Eastern" in McGinn et al., eds., *Christian Spirituality*, 401.

internal insight."[26] Symeon the New Theologian writes of *moving* or relocating the mind to the heart: "The mind should be in the heart . . . Keep your mind there (in the heart), trying by every possible means to find the place where the heart is, in order that, having found it, your mind should constantly abide there. Wrestling thus, your mind will find the place of the heart."[27]

The heart represents an awareness of the Divine in a wide range of traditions. The writer of Ephesians had prayed: "with the eyes of your heart enlightened, you may know what is the hope to which he has called you, what are the riches of his glorious inheritance among the saints" (1:18). Augustine experienced an inner listlessness: "our hearts are restless 'til they rest in You."[28] Benedict's *Rule* begins with the words, "Listen carefully, my son, to the master's instructions and attend to them with the ear of your heart."[29] Richard Baxter's hymn invites us to "with a well tuned heart sing thou the songs of love" while Charles Wesley pens the great hymn beginning: "O for a heart to praise my God."

How is the heart celebrated in the expressions of spirituality we have discovered?

The Kabbalah tradition reminded us of the need to maintain and safeguard *kavanah*—the true intention of the heart and mind in prayer. This involves both the emotional and the intellectual— involving a focused concentration and devotion. Dalia told us: *"What we all need is an open heart; that enables us to hear the reality of the Other. The open heart opens the way to miracles . . . When we really listen—not having our prepared answers—we can overcome the negative energy that comes from prejudice . . . It all comes from the heart. We need to expand the heart, enlarge it: this can be a painful process and takes time. But Isaiah says [54:2]: "Enlarge the site of your tent, and let the curtains of your habitations be stretched out;*

---

26. Archimandrite Ephraim of Vatopedi Monastery, "The Soul and Repentance" in Friends of Mount Athos, *Annual Report 2006*.

27. Attributed to Symeon the New Theologian, "Three Methods of Attention and Prayer," in Kadloubovsky and Palmer, trans., *Writings*, 158.

28. Augustine of Hippo, *Confessions* (trans. Chadwick), 3.

29. Benedict of Nursa, *Rule of Benedict in English* (trans. Fry), 15.

do not hold back; lengthen your cords and strengthen your stakes."
He was talking of the tent of your heart.[30]

In the Sufi tradition Sheikh Ahram reminded us: "*Sufis are interested in regular religious practices but the key aim is to draw the Name of God into the heart. We progress to* iman *where fear turns to love, and our practice becomes more interior, in the heart. But we are aiming at* ihsan. *We begin to get a feeling of God. We follow the way of God. We realize that God sees everything. He looks into the heart.*" A key theme is that the heart is the locus of the Divine. Farid reminded us that we do not have to look far for the Divine:

> Why roam the jungle with thorns pricking your feet?
>
> Your Lord is in your heart, you wander hoping Him you'll meet! . . .
>
> Don't look in wilderness or to a bed of thorns take . . .
>
> That One isn't outside, in your heart is One, awake!
>
> In every heart God's living, so don't hurt any heart . . .[31]

One commentator explains:

> The heart (*qalb*), though connected in some mysterious way with the physical heart, is not a thing of flesh and blood. Unlike the English "heart," its nature is rather intellectual than emotional, but whereas the intellect cannot gain real knowledge of God, the *qalb* is capable of knowing the essences of all things, and when illumined by faith and knowledge reflects the whole content of the divine mind; hence the Prophet said, "My earth and My heaven contain Me not, but the heart of My faithful servant containeth Me."[32]

The heart itself is a doorway, a gateway, that might permit entry to sensory illusions or to divine insights. As Rumi said, "Here a world and there a world . . . I am seated on the threshold."[33]

30. Dalia Landau (founder of Open House in Ramle), interview by Andrew Mayes, July 2011 at St George's College in Jerusalem

31. Smith, trans., *Baba Farid,* 50, 138.

32. Quoted in Nicholson, *Mystics,* 68.

33. Quoted in Nicholson, *Mystics,* 69.

If in the different traditions the heart is the mystical center of a person, Syriac writers remind us that what is sought most of all is a compassionate heart. Isaac the Syrian puts it like this:

> What is a compassionate heart? . . . It is a heart on fire for the whole of creation, for humanity, for the birds, for the animals, for demons and for all that exists. At the recollection and at the sight of them such a person's eyes overflow with tears owing to the strength of the compassion which grips his heart; as a result of his deep mercy his heart shrinks and cannot bear to hear or look on any injury or the slightest suffering of anything in creation. That is why he constantly offers up prayer full of tears, even for the irrational animals and for the enemies of truth, even for those who harm him, so that they may be protected and find mercy . . . he prays as a result of the great compassion which is poured out beyond measure—after the likeness of God—in his heart.[34]

Such words lead us to take a look at the relationship between interior prayer and action in the world.

The Mystical and the Prophetic: A Great Divide?

Sometimes spirituality gets bad press. Attentiveness to our individual and personal spiritual journey can be regarded as self-indulgent, fostering a spirituality that is introverted, narcisstic, self-centered, closed in on itself. Is it about escapism and navel-gazing and encouraging insularity? Does spirituality provide a refuge from life's storms, a place of safety away from the harsh realities of life? Is it a distraction from, or evasion of, reality? Does it represent a flight from the world? A diversion to keep us peaceful, to insulate us and keep free from stress? Does the practice of prayer amount to luxuriating in self-absorption, spiritual pleasure seeking? Does it encourage living in an ivory tower—or burying one's head in the sand? Perceptions give fuel to this critique: spirituality is seen as a ghettoized, personal matter, a private concern, nurturing the inner

34. Isaac, Bishop of Nineveh, *Ascetical Homilies*, 344.

world at the expense of the outer: for Christians, it is about "me and Jesus." People sometimes talk of spirituality in terms of self-fulfillment or self-discovery, the exploration of the "spiritual side of themselves." It has been called "another bandwagon to jump on, or a market need to satisfy."[35] Pope Francis calls us in his apostolic exhortation *Evangelii Gaudium* to radiate the joy of the gospel and develop an outgoing, outward-looking missionary spirituality. He observes:

> Today we are seeing in many pastoral workers . . . an inordinate concern for their personal freedom and relaxation . . . At the same time, the spiritual life comes to be identified with a few religious exercises which can offer a certain comfort but which do not encourage encounter with others, engagement with the world or a passion for evangelization.

He continues:

> Mystical notions without a solid social and missionary outreach are of no help to evangelization . . . What is needed is the ability to cultivate an interior space which can give a Christian meaning to commitment and activity.[36]

The danger is that spirituality becomes as an esoteric and fringe activity, for those spiritual and heavenly minded beings among us that perhaps have too much time on their hands! The focus becomes pandering to the ego and self-development. The all-pervasive individualism which infects so much of Western society, allied to a consumerist approach to all things ("what can I get out of this; what's in this for me?"), can seep into how people approach spirituality. Spirituality can become a hobby, a recreational activity for self-entertainment. God becomes a private experience. Post-modernist thinking has reinforced the divide between private and public and considers spirituality, and indeed religion, as something

35. Freeman, "Dangers of the shallow end."

36. Pope Francis, *Evangelii Gaudium*, 46, 128.

that pertains only to the subjective, private lives of individuals. Philip Sheldrake observes:

> If human solidarity is forgotten, contemplation becomes no more than spiritual self-delusion. A non-social experience, or one that is purely "spiritual" and removed from our material existence, is a self-centered concern for a false peace. The greatest danger for Christian spirituality is for it to become anti-material, spiritualized, and individualistic . . . There will be a tendency to retreat into prayer and "spiritual" experiences as ends in themselves without any obvious implications for our behavior and attitudes . . . Prayer that is unconcerned with the situation of our neighbor is pure self-indulgence.[37]

Eugene Peterson notes that "every expression of spirituality, left to itself, tends towards being more about me and less about God."[38] Saint John says, "Those who do not love a brother or sister whom they have seen, cannot love God whom they have not seen" (1 John 4:20). James is emphatic: "Show me your faith apart from your works, and I by my works will show you my faith" (2:18).

The Christian religion proclaims: "The Word became flesh and dwelt among us" (John 1:14, RSV). God is to be found in the stable, the marketplace, the cross. But from the beginning there has been a tendency in Christian thinking to spiritualize the physical. In his version of the Lord's Prayer, Luke turns Matthew's "Release us from our debts" (Matt 6:12, my translation)—a physical petition arising from a situation of dire material poverty—into "Forgive us our sins" (Luke 11:4), In the Beatitudes, Matthew spiritualizes Luke's "Blessed are you poor" (Luke 6:20, my translation) into "Blessed are the poor in spirit" (Matt 5:3). It is often easier to conceive of spiritual things instead of getting our hands dirty. We forget that the root meaning of the very word "ministry," *diakonia*, means "through the dust." The flesh of God forbids any retreat into "spiritual religion."

---

37. Sheldrake, *Images*, 92, 93. 94.
38. Peterson, *Christ Plays*, 47.

An incarnational spirituality celebrates not only God within, but God in our very midst, in the dirt and in the gutter, where the prayer of contemplation must of necessity lead to courageous and compassionate action. Prayer might begin with a sense of God beyond: "Our Father who art in heaven." But it dares to pray "thy kingdom come" and moves to an awareness of the God nearby: "Thy will be done on earth as it is in heaven."

But Christian spirituality became infected with divisive, dualistic thinking from the time in the early centuries when theologians embraced Platonic thought. Plato himself wrote in the *Republic* that attentiveness to the world of the senses was "looking in the wrong direction."[39] The key to life was to become radically detached from the concerns of the body. Disastrous polarities crept into Christian thinking, undermining the idea of God's incarnation. Things were pitched against one another: heaven was opposed to earth, the body to the spirit. Politics and prayer were to be kept separate. Sacred and secular were delineated as if they were two separate realms—holy and unholy. The church and the world are set against each other. Such dualistic thinking creates unnecessary distances and opens up uncalled for chasms. When God is thought of as "up there," prayer becomes detached from life.[40] Throughout the history of Christian spirituality, the contemplative life has been exalted above the active apostolate. Thomas Aquinas

39. Plato, *Republic,* 518 quoted in Louth, *Origins,* 6.

40. In the spiritual classics, images of ascent to God predominate: the further we get up the mountain of prayer, leaving the earth behind, the closer we get to God. The further the earth below, the greater the proximity to God. A flight from the world is required. Many spiritual writers see prayer as a "going up" to God: John Climacus (579–649), abbot of the of Saint Catherine's Monastery at the foot of Mount Sinai itself, suggested in his work *The Ladder of Divine Ascent* that there were thirty rungs on the staircase to heaven, thirty virtues to be nurtured. Saint Bonaventure (1217–1274) in *The Journey of the Mind into God* writes of the "mind's ascent to God." In the English tradition, Walter Hilton (d. 1396) described prayer in terms of ascending a *Ladder of Perfection,* the title of his major work. John of the Cross centers his masterpiece *The Ascent of Mount Carmel* on the model of going up to God in prayer. A recurring theme is the necessity for detachment—withdrawal from daily demands in order to enter prayer, conceived as a sacred space, as a different world.

in his *Summa Theologiae* (question 182) gives eight reasons why the angelic life of prayer is a higher calling and attracts more merit than the active life of service. Counsels of perfection encouraged an elitist view of spirituality, for those who were able to make withdrawal from the world.

Robert McAfee Brown subtitled his book *Spirituality and Liberation* with the words, *Overcoming the Great Fallacy.*[41] He identifies this as a persistent dualism that separates and opposes faith and ethics, the holy and the profane, the otherworldly and this-worldly—eroding the central Christian belief in the Word made flesh. Encounter with the Divine changes people and makes a measurable difference to their lives. The late Methodist scholar Gordon Wakefield stresses this: "Spirituality concerns the way in which prayer influences conduct, our behavior and manner of life, our attitudes to other people . . . Spirituality is the combination of living and praying."[42] Dyckman and Carroll suggest, "Spirituality is the style of a person's response to Christ before the challenge of everyday life, in a given historical and cultural environment."[43] Leech puts it like this:

> I believe that we can speak of spirituality as a necessary bedrock and foundation of our lives, provided that we understand that we are speaking of the foundation and not of a compartment. To speak of spirituality in this sense is to speak of the whole life of the human person and human community in their relationship with the Divine.[44]

Privatized spirituality is a contradiction in terms. Spirituality—the encounter with God—is the wellspring of mission and witness in the world. The encounter with God is not to be kept as some private possession but rather should energize and stimulate our life of witness. Prayer should lead us to that risky place where we engage with the struggle for justice and where we are ready to

41. Brown, *Spirituality.*
42. Wakefield, *Dictionary,* v.
43. Dyckman and Carroll, *Inviting the Mystic,* 79.
44. Leech, *Eye of the Storm,* 16.

speak out for our faith. Mary needs Martha; the disciple becomes the apostle; love of God spills over to love of neighbor. As Richard Rohr reminds us, it is both/and not either/or.[45]

Spirituality needs to experience repeatedly a shift from the inward to the outward, and where necessary, vice versa. Jesus calls us: "whenever you pray, go into your room and shut the door and pray to your Father who is in secret" (Matt 6:6). But we also need to open the door to mission—as Paul puts it, "A wide door for effective work has opened to me, and there are many adversaries" (1 Cor 16:9); and "God will open to us a door for the word, that we may declare the mystery of Christ" (Col 4:3). There is a time for closing of doors, and flinging them wide.

Contemporary spirituality needs to be alert to the criticism that it can become elitist and individualistic, fostering a "personal relationship with God" at the expense of an incarnate spirituality grounded and earthed in the needs of the age and aware of the danger of what Gerald W. Hughes calls "split spirituality"—piety that has become adrift from life.[46] Just as Thomas Merton, the contemplative within a Cistercian/Trappist tradition, came to see the role of the monk as a social critic, so we must acknowledge that our spiritual relationship needs to be rooted within the demands and struggles of the world. Merton wrote in 1963: "What is the contemplative life if one doesn't listen to God in it? What is the contemplative life if one becomes oblivious to the rights of men [and women] and the truth of God in the world and in His Church?"[47] He goes on: "We do not go into the desert [of prayer] to escape people but to learn how to find them; we do not leave them in order to have nothing more to do with them, but to find out the way to do them most good."[48]

As Kenneth Leech reminds us, "all spirituality must be judged by the vision of the coming age. The Kingdom is the standard by

45. Rohr, *Naked Now*; Rohr, *Everything Belongs*.

46. Hughes, *God in All Things*, ch. 1.

47. Letter to Daniel Berrigan quoted in Shannon, *"Something of a Rebel,"* 108.

48. Merton, *New Seeds*, 80.

which the Christian disciple lives, and by that standard he discerns the signs of the times."[49] There can be no place for individualistic spirituality in the context of living in a community in conflict with political or commercial powers, where the experience of struggle is a daily reality. Jim Wallis laments and affirms:

> Personal piety has become an end in itself instead of the energy for social justice . . . Prophetic spirituality will always fundamentally challenge the system at its roots and offer genuine alternatives based on values from our truest religious, cultural and political traditions.[50]

Mystical prayer, then—the sort of prayer that is utterly open to God, that is receptive and perceptive—leads to the prophetic: taking a stand against social injustices and responding coura- geously to the needs of those who hurt, near and far.

Inside/out in the Traditions We Have Encountered

One of the most striking and consistent commonalities we en- countered in the diversity of traditions is how the practice of prayer leads to action in the world.

Rabbi Mendel Osdoba was emphatic: *"We serve God in all places, not just in the synagogue. But all the time. Outside and inside must match—what goes on in the heart and what goes on in the body and the world. Some people say they are spiritual on the inside but secular on the outside. But that is a false division and dichotomy."*[51] And we noted, how in Kabbalah the concept of *tikkun*, repairing the world, relates mystic prayer to action in a very intentional way.

Sheikh Ahram was very clear: *"The key feeling, as I said, is to love God and to be filled with love, and to carry this into our daily life. The people who fight in the streets need to get this knowledge.*

---

49. Leech, *Soul Friend,* 190.

50. Wallis, *Soul of Politics,* 38, 47.

51. Rabbi Mendel Osdoba, interview with Andrew Mayes in August 2011 at Chabad House

Hate blocks. Love opens . . . You see, the ceremony in the mosque leads to life in the world, it leads to peace, rest, respect."[52]

Greek patriarch Theophilos echoed such sentiments: *"You reveal what is happening on the inside by what comes out. You see, what goes on the mind—the Logos—the Word of God, this is an inner reality and thought but it comes out in so many ways. It comes out in the spoken greeting "Christos Aneste! Christ is risen!" But is comes out most in our lives, living with courage and hope in the heart of the city."*[53]

But the problem persists and is an ever-present danger. Daoud, on the Via Dolorosa, told us: *"The pilgrims on the street don't often stop to buy anything from my shop here. They keep their heads down in their prayerbooks and beads—they are so caught up in their devotions they don't seem even to notice us. They don't stop to speak to us! Christians need to open their eyes!"*[54] If the pilgrims were more alert to the very environs and context of their prayer on the Way of the Cross they would notice soldiers hassling Arab teenagers, marginalized refugees attending the workshop for the blind at the fifth station, women like Aneesa sitting in the gutter selling herbs. As we observed in chapter 6, the Via Dolorosa invites us to discover glimpses of God in the faces of those who suffer in our very midst today, to touch the Divine in the brokenness of hurting lives.

On the Damascus Road

Let's consider another example of the interplay between outer and inner. The address of St. George's Anglican Cathedral is, Damascus Road, Jerusalem. The distance from Jerusalem to Damascus is about one hundred and fifty miles. Saint George's Cathedral is

---

52. Sheikh Mazen Ahram (inspector of the Al-Aqsa Mosque), interview by Andrew Mayes in June 2014 at St George's College in Jerusalem.

53. His Beatitude Patriarch Theophilos III (patriarch of the Holy City of Jerusalem and all Palestine and Israel), interview by Andrew Mayes in November 2010 at the Greek Orthodox Patriarchate in Jerusalem

54. Daoud (Arab shopkeeper), interview by Andrew Mayes in December 2010.

located right on Damascus Road, just a mile from the Damascus Gate on the north side of the Old City of Jerusalem. The Cathedral is the mother church of the diocese, which serves Syria, Lebanon, and Jordan besides parishes in the State of Israel and in the West Bank. Its ministry of healthcare and education serves all, regardless of religious affiliation: St. George's School, next door on Damascus Road, is a Christian institution with 98 percent Muslim students. The diocesan peace and reconciliation department strengthens relationships by means of interfaith dialogue with Jews and Muslims; a monthly gathering also takes place here on Damascus Road. Archbishop Suheil Dawani reflects on how celebration of worship spills over to the needs around:[55]

> The mission of the church here in the Holy City of Jerusalem and throughout the Holy Land continues to be focused in building bridges of peace and reconciliation rooted in the love of God for all his children.
>
> With the resurrection our faith is renewed to greater commitment to the mission of the church. It is both a pastoral presence and as a faithful witness through which God's love may be experienced by all of our neighbors, no matter their religious beliefs. The mission of Christ is to love all people, not to condemn, but to love. The mission of the church here continues to be a source of God's love shining the light of hope through our parishes, schools, hospitals and clinics.
>
> The source of our celebration is and must always remain in the power of the resurrection faith of Easter morning. This is the day which defeated, once and for all, the power of death and grave to control the lives of faithful people. Our faith is renewed in the shadow of the empty cross. Our commitment finds new courage as we look into the empty tomb. Our hope for the future is strong for it is the love of God in Christ Jesus which fills our hearts.

Such testimonies raise big questions about own spirituality and prayer. Are there danger signs that my spirituality is becoming

55. Bishop (now Archbishop) Suheil Dawani (Episcopal Diocese of Jerusalem), Easter Message, April 2011.

narcissistic, self-centered, closed in on itself? Is my spirituality about self-fulfillment or about empowering sacrificial living? If the measure of spiritual maturity is increasing solidarity with the hurting, an enlarging capacity for compassion, what are the signs that I am maturing? Is my heart getting bigger? How far can I allow the pain of the world to enter my prayer? Does my prayer have room for the oppressions and injustices of the world? What place is there for a costly intercession inseparable from self-offering (that does not let me "off the hook")? If I stand in the Christian tradition, I might ask: What place is there in my prayer for the cross—not only in terms of seeking personal forgiveness but in terms of realizing that God suffers among us? What does Matthew 25 look like in my experience? What is the evidence? Am I drawn to the margins in any way?

As we reflect on the various testimonies we have received, we are impressed by the creative interrelationship between prayer and practice, between contemplation and action, between seeking solitude and the call to build community, between stillness and activity. We see how a healthy spirituality, in whatever expression, has the potential to inspire, energize, shape and reshape, reorder, stimulate, and renew vision and engagement with the Other. Now the Jaffa Gate beckons us, with its challenge to take out into a hurting world our own discoveries of the Divine.

Questions for Reflection

1. What insight strikes you and inspires you from a tradition other than your own?

2. How does this resonate with your own tradition or challenge it?

3. How does your inner life of spirituality impact your outer life of action and engagement?

4. How would you describe your experience of the relationship and interaction between the inner and outer, between the mystical and the prophetic?

5. In what ways can you discern evidences and signs of divinization in others and in yourself?

Prayer Exercise

Use your hands expressively in this prayer-time in four actions.

Begin by clenching your fists tight and holding them before you. Feel the tension and let these fists represent an anger or frustration that bothers you today, a situation in the world that you feel strongly about. Hold them before God in the solidarity of prayer and intercession.

Secondly, slowly open your down-turned palms and let go of the tension. Let it fall away from you to God. In this gesture give to God any negative feelings or stresses, feel them drip out of your fingertips, as it were. Surrender the situation to God's providence and sovereignty.

Thirdly, turn your hands upwards in a gesture of surrender to God and of receiving from God. Breathe in what God wants to give you right now – perhaps a reassurance that all will be well. Breathe in his empowering Spirit who will give you the courage for action.

Finally, take a look at your hands. Is there an action that God is calling you to make in relation to your initial concern? What should you do as a result of this – something bold, something risky or rebellious?

End with the Serenity Prayer: 'God grant me the serenity to accept the things I cannot change; courage to change the things I can; and wisdom to know the difference.'

Further Reading

Wingate, Andrew. *Celebrating Difference, Staying Faithful: How to Live in a Multi-faith World.* London: Darton, Longman & Todd, 2005.

FIGURE 8

8

From the Jaffa Gate

Embracing a Hurting World

THE WIDE WEST-FACING JAFFA Gate stands next to the Citadel (known as the Tower of David). The gate takes its name from the fact that from it roads lead out to the wider world. It is the place where pilgrims arrive, and the place from which they depart—pointing to the ancient seaport of Jaffa, known in the Bible as Joppa, the port Jonah left to begin his mission (Jonah 1:3). It orients us toward the Mediterranean coast—and also, in modern times, toward the airport from which pilgrims leave the country, moving out into the world. It invites us to reflect as we return to our usual worlds: how am I changed? How have my perceptions or spiritual practices shifted or grown? What is the next step on my journey?

It is significant that the apostle Peter's horizons were massively expanded at Jaffa. Not only did he physically look out on the beckoning western seas, but also through a remarkable vision, related in Acts 10 and 11, he gained a breadth of perspective echoed in Frederick W. Faber's well-known 1862 hymn: "There's a wideness in God's mercy / like the wideness of the sea." Peter realized that he can call no animal or human unclean or unacceptable. He testifies: "I truly understand that God shows no partiality, but in every nation anyone who fears him and does what is right is acceptable to him" (Acts 10:34–35). The NIV translates it this way: "I now realize how true it is that God does not show favoritism." Peter immediately lives out this insight, for the account goes on (11:12): "The Spirit told me to go with them and not to make a distinction between them and us."

Thus the Jaffa and the gate named after it calls us to an expansiveness of vision, and summons us to ask ourselves if our vison is too narrow. In fact the very gate itself confronts us with a choice. It was widened in the nineteenth century to receive and send out VIPs and other travelers, so it's now spacious and welcoming, though the old narrow Ottoman gate persists at the side, a symbol of constricted and defensive thinking. Which gate will we choose?

Significantly, the Arabic name for the gate is Bab al-Khalil, Gate of the Friend, because the southerly road from it leads to Hebron, the burial place of Abraham, whom Scripture hails as "the friend of God." The Letter of James (2:23) puts it this way: "the scripture was fulfilled which says, 'Abraham believed God, and it was reckoned to him as righteousness'; and he was called the friend of God." James was quoting from God's words relayed by the prophet: "But you, Israel, my servant, / . . . / the offspring of Abraham, my friend" (Isa 41:8, compare 2 Chr 20:7). This is echoed in the Qur'an: "Who can be better in religion than one who submits his whole self to Allah, does good, and follows the way of Abraham the true in Faith? For Allah did take Abraham for a friend" (Qur'an, sura 4).[1]

So this gate reminds us of Abraham, our father in faith, and prompts us to recall not only his remarkable friendship with God but also his big-hearted capacity for friendship with strangers. Abraham is a towering archetypal figure who can still inspire us today and we can learn much from his example. As we stand at his gate, preparing to return to our worlds of engagement, Abraham, father to the three monotheistic religions we have explored in this book, lays before us a fourfold challenge:

---

1. The translation is by Abdullah Yusuf Ali (corpus.quran.com) (http://corpus.quran.com/translation.jsp?chapter=4&verse=125/).

Seek Utter Openness to the Divine

Abraham is celebrated, first and foremost as a person of unquestioning faith. Abraham becomes "the ancestor of all who believe" (Rom 4:11). He is astonishingly open to the Divine, even when God utters or commands things that are puzzling, unfathomable, seemingly impossible. "What then are we to say was gained by Abraham, our ancestor according to the flesh? . . . For what does the scripture say? 'Abraham believed God, and it was reckoned to him as righteousness'" (Rom 4:1, 3). Abraham believed the promise of a son though such a birth was inconceivable in every sense. Later, he was even willing to offer Isaac, the son of promise, when God demanded it (Heb 11:17–19). The kind of faith that Abraham models for us is unconditional trust and total availability to God—involving an ability to listen to God, to discover the Divine, to stay open to surprises and to the unexpected. Genesis chapter 15 affords examples. God might be discovered in a mystical vision (15:1). The truth might reveal itself in the stars: "The LORD brought him outside and said, 'Look toward heaven and count the stars, if you are able to count them'" (15:5). The Divine might be encountered in the darkness: "As the sun was going down, a deep sleep fell upon Abram, and a deep and terrifying darkness descended upon him. Then the LORD said to Abram, 'Know this for certain . . . ' When the sun had gone down and it was dark, a smoking fire pot and a flaming torch passed between these pieces [of the sacrifice]. On that day the LORD made a covenant with Abram . . ." (15:12–13, 17–18). Abraham calls out to us across five millennia: "rule nothing out—if you seek the Divine!"

Keep a Pilgrim Heart

By faith Abraham obeyed when he was called to set out for a place that he was to receive as an inheritance; and by faith he stayed for a time in the land he had been promised, as in a foreign land, living in tents. For he

> looked forward to the city that has foundations, whose
> architect and builder is God. (Heb 11:8–10)

He was prepared to move—physically and spiritually. Genesis 12 tells us "Now the Lord said to Abram, 'Go from your country and your kindred and your father's house to the land that I will show you.'" He was prepared to quit his comfort zone, leave behind his home, and venture forth on a journey into the unknown. He was prepared to let go of his familiar securities, even his cherished inherited concepts of God, and move out on a journey of faith: "he set out, not knowing where he was going" (Heb 11:8). Abraham truly had a pilgrim heart, or as the English poet of the seventeenth century from the Anglican tradition, George Herbert, put it: "a heart in pilgrimage." He was prepared to live with vulnerability and risk, quitting his comfortable stone house, ready to be "living in tents" (Heb 11:9).

In the course of this book, we have begun a journey, we have set out together, and now we must keep moving. We have not arrived. We must be prepared, like Abraham himself, to let go sometimes of conventions and concepts that would pull us back and tie us down. We must be prepared, as it were, to "live in tents"—to live with the provisional, the impermanent, the uncomfortable, the unsettling, for as long as it takes. We do not know the outcome of our journey, but God does. Let's pledge to keep on walking, though many would discourage us. God calls us to keep moving forwards as companions on the journey—Jewish, Muslim and Christian, as children of Abraham. Let us pray for the faith of Abraham to grow in our own hearts, an unshakable trust in God, the God of our journey. Paul puts it this way:

> There is no longer Jew or Greek, there is no longer slave
> or free, there is no longer male and female . . . you are
> Abraham's offspring, heirs according to the promise.
> (Gal 3:28).

Extend Hospitality to the Other and to the Stranger

The inspirational story of the gracious hospitality of Abraham is related in Genesis 18:

> He looked up and saw three men standing near him. When he saw them, he ran from the tent entrance to meet them, and bowed down to the ground. He said, "My lord, if I find favor with you, do not pass by your servant. Let a little water be brought, and wash your feet, and rest yourselves under the tree. Let me bring a little bread, that you may refresh yourselves, and after that you may pass on—since you have come to your servant." (Gen 18: 2–5)

Abraham exemplifies a capacity to welcome the stranger. For him, this turns out to be a life-changing encounter with the Divine. He is prepared to accept the stranger into his midst unconditionally, anticipating the call of God through the prophet Isaiah:

> Enlarge the site of your tent,
>> and let the curtains of your habitations be stretched out;
> do not hold back; lengthen your cords
>> and strengthen your stakes (Isa 54:2).

No wonder he was hailed as "friend of God."

Take Risks in Friendship

In situations where strife could have occurred and then escalated, Abraham seemed able to defuse them. He emerges as a peacemaker. His unselfish nature is not only seen in giving his nephew Lot first choice of land in which to pasture his flocks and herds (Gen 13:9). It reveals itself also in his readiness and determination to intercede for the condemned people of Sodom and Gomorrah (Gen 18:16–33). He did what he could to spare them from impending judgment.

Abraham's relationship with the Philistine warlord Abimelech was at first, according to Genesis 20, fraught and full of suspicion and tension. In Gen 21:25–34 we read of Abraham's argument with

Abimelech, whose servants seized control of a well of water Abraham was using. But Abraham takes some creative steps forward to heal the fractured relationship. He resolves the dispute and avoids further conflict by entering into a covenant with Abimelech, sealing the agreement by his gift to him of seven lambs, which gives the well the name Beer-sheba, meaning "the well of the oath." In this Abraham reveals a capacity for reconciliation and risk. His covenant or agreement with the Other is the first recorded in Scripture and encourages us to take risks that might lead to deeper mutual understanding and even friendship, deepening trust and openness.

The narrative concludes: "Abraham planted a tamarisk tree in Beer-sheba, and called there on the name of the Lord, the Everlasting God. And Abraham resided as an alien many days in the land of the Philistines" (Gen 21:33,34). He was prepared to abide for a significant amount of time in a foreign land as a sojourner, stranger, pilgrim. He was ready for the long haul, and was not going away—he displays a determination, a tenacity to remain in a place where he will encounter those of different traditions around him, in the hope that the Other will become Brother. Friend of God is prepared to become friend to all Others.

How can you support neighbors of other traditions, or spiritual searchers, from the treasures of your own spiritual tradition? What have you got to share? What questions are they asking? What are they seeking, searching for? Dare you take steps forward in initiating relationships that might bloom into friendship? Christ suggests clues in the building of spiritual friendships. As Jesus laid on the bosom of the Father (John 1:18), so he invites his beloved disciple to place his head on own his breast (John 13:23). Such friendship is characterized by a confiding of secrets, an unabashed sharing of discoveries: "I do not call you servants any longer, because the servant does not know what the master is doing; but I have called you friends, because I have made known to you everything I have heard from my Father" (John 15:15). Across the three monotheistic religions we already enjoy a spiritual kinship, a sense of family: we have much to build on, much to share.

In today's world marked by transient, shifting populations, mobility, and displacement, we find ourselves in close proximity to the Other. What different spiritual traditions can you discover in your own context? What contact do you have with them? How can you take risky steps to engage with them? What thresholds do you need to cross? What gateways to the Divine are to be found in your very neighborhood?

Questions for Reflection

1. In what ways can you extend or develop hospitality or welcome to the Other, in your own context? What steps forward can you make in this area?

2. As you survey the journey of this book, what stands out for you as the most striking insight?

3. What stands out for you as the greatest challenge?

4. What creative steps forward can you take in forging interfaith friendships?

5. Recall the words in the Letter to the Hebrews: "Therefore Jesus also suffered outside the city gate in order to sanctify the people by his own blood. Let us then go to him outside the camp and bear the abuse he endured. For here we have no lasting city, but we are looking for the city that is to come" (13:12–14). What awaits you "outside the city gate"?

Prayer Exercise

Pray with Andrei Rublev's icon of the Hospitality of Abraham painted (or written) in 1425. It depicts the story of Abraham entertaining three angels (Gen 18), representing the persons of the Trinity See this Wikipedia page: https://en.wikipedia.org/wiki/Trinity_(Andrei_Rublev)/. For another version, which depicts in addition the figures of Abraham and Sarah, see the image here:

https://commons.wikimedia.org/wiki/File:Hospitality_of_Abraham_(Zakynthos_15th_c.,_Byzantine_museum).jpg/. Through line and color the iconographer seeks to convey a sense of awe and mystery, and to stimulate prayer. Colors are significant: blue stands for heaven; green signifies earth; red represents human flesh; purple suggests power; white represents purity or light; and gold signals divine energy or the glory of God.

Notice in particular the gap and open space at the front of the icon: it invites the viewer to become a participant in the shared meal, and to join the angels at the table. (Rublev's original, two meters square, in the Tretyakov Museum in Moscow, enables a person standing in front of it to be fully incorporated in the encounter with the Divine—one finds oneself actually included in the meal and in the embrace of the angels!) As you reflect on the four challenges of Abraham and on your journey through the gateways of Jerusalem, consider prayerfully how you can open up such a welcoming space to the Other in your own life.

Further Reading

Peters, F. E. *The Children of Abraham: Judaism, Christianity, Islam.* Princeton Classic Editions. Princeton University Press, 2006.

Appendix

OUR INTERFAITH GROUP IN Jerusalem consisted of two or three Christians and the same number of Jews and Muslims—about nine people in total. Each was asked to select a piece of work to share with the group: this could be a reading from Scripture, a poem or a piece of prose; it could even be a picture or an art object. Initial reactions to the chosen piece of work were shared—i.e., what it means to each person; and then more engaging "responses from the heart" were shared, forming part of a gentle discussion, during which people were able to speak freely. We had a sense that a sacred space opened up in the course of our hour's meeting. Here is the "Mutual Invitation Format" used in Jerusalem interfaith gatherings:

1. The leader has chosen a short reading from sacred Scripture, or from spiritual writing, or a poem.

2. The leader reads the chosen work aloud.

3. The leader invites someone (it needn't be in any particular order) to respond with a word or phrase which is their initial response to the reading. They do not explain or justify their choice to the group, and the group does not remark or question this word. They simply listen. The first speaker then invites the response of another group member until all who wish have spoken. Anyone can pass at any time if they are not ready to share a word or phrase for whatever reason. It is not necessary to explain why. The leader responds last.

4. The text is read again, this time by a second member of the group. The original leader will add a specific question to reflect on concerning the text. It could simply be a general question such as, What insights come up for you? Or, what does this text say to us today in our present situation?

5. The reader invites another group member to respond. This should be a relatively short (one- or two-minute) response from the heart, not a theological dissertation. (At this time, there is to be no interruption or discussion. Everyone simply listens to one another. Nevertheless, if the whole group agrees that it is a good idea, then a discussion can continue following this initial reflection.) If someone goes on and on, the leader of the entire exercise can gently remind the person of time restraints. The leader should give their reflections last since they are likely most familiar with the text.

6. The text is read for a third and final time by a new person. This time it is read as a prayer, and the group simply listens to the reading.

See also www.scripturalreasoning.org/ and Ford and Pecknold, eds., *Promise of Scriptural Reasoning.*

Bibliography

Adamson, Daniel Silas. "Jerusalem's 800-year-old Indian Hospice." *BBC News Magazine*, 23 November 2014. https://www.bbc.com/news/magazine-30122030/.

Alfeyev, Hilarion. *The Spiritual World of Isaac the Syrian*. Cistersican Studies Series 175. Kalamazoo, MI: Cistercian, 2000.

Arberry A. J., ed. *The Rubáiyát of Omar Khayyaám and Other Persian Poems: An Anthology of Verse Translations*. Everyman's Library 1996. London: Dutton, 1972.

Armstrong, Karen. *Jerusalem: One City, Three Faiths*. New York: Knopf, 1996.

Armstrong, Regis J., et al., eds. *Francis of Assisi: Early Documents*. 2 vols. New York: New City, 1999–2000.

Association for Civil Rights in Israel. "East Jerusalem—Facts and Figures." May 2019. Webpage. https://www.english.acri.org.il/east-jerusalem-2019/.

Ateek, Naim Stifan. *Contemporary Way of the Cross*. Jerusalem: Sabeel Ecumenical Liberation Center, 2005.

————. *A Palestinian Christian Cry for Reconciliation*. Maryknoll, NY: Orbis, 2008.

Augustine of Hippo. *Confessions*. Translated by Henry Chadwick. Oxford World's Classics. Oxford: Oxford University Press 1991.

Basil, Bishop of Caesarea. *On the Holy Spirit*. In *Saint Basil: Letters and Select Works*, edited by Henry Wace and Philip Schaff, 1–50. A Select Library of the Nicene and Post-Nicene Fathers, 2nd ser., 8. Reprint, London: Forgotten Books, 2016.

Benedict, Abbot of Monte Cassino. *The Rule of St. Benedict in English*. Translated by Timothy Fry. Collegeville, MN: Liturgical, 1982.

Bielecki, Tessa. *Teresa of Avila: An Introduction to Her Life and Writings*. London: Burns & Oates, 1994.

Bokser, Ben Zion. *The Jewish Mystical Tradition*. Northvale, NJ: Aronson, 1993.

Bourgeault, Cynthia. *The Wisdom Jesus: Transforming Heart and Mind; A New Perspective on Christ and His Message*. Boston: New Seeds, 2008.

Brock, Sebastian P., trans. *The Luminous Eye: The Spiritual World Vision of Saint Ephrem.* Rev. ed. Cistercian Studies Series 124. Kalamazoo, MI: Cistercian, 1992.

———, trans. *The Syriac Fathers on Prayer and the Spiritual Life.* Cistercian Studies Series 101. Kalamazoo, MI: Cisterican, 1987.

Brother Ramon, SSF. *Franciscan Spirituality: Following St Francis Today.* London: SPCK, 2008.

Brown, Robert McAfee. *Spirituality and Liberation: Overcoming the Great Fallacy.* Philadelphia: Westminster, 1988.

Carretto, Carlo. *I, Francis: The Spirit of St. Francis of Assisi.* London: Collins, 1982.

Center for Jewish Spirituality. "Amidah: The Silent Prayer." http://iyyun.com/teachings/amidah-the-silent-prayer.

Charry, Ellen T. *By the Renewing of Your Minds: The Pastoral Function of Christian Doctrine.* Oxford: Oxford University Press, 1997.

Chopra, Deepak, ed. *The Love Poems of Rumi.* Translated by Deepak Chopra and Fereydoun Kia. London: Rider, 1998.

Church Union. *Order for the Eucharist 2015.* London: Tufton, 2015.

Cordovero, Moses ben Jacob. *The Palm Tree of Devorah.* Translated and annotated by Moshe Miller. Southfield, MI: Targum, 1993.

———. "Soul Meditation: Linking One's Awareness to the Divine, in Prayer." Meditation and Prayer. Jewish Meditation. Kaballah Online. *Chabad.* https://www.chabad.org/Kabbalah/article_cdo/aid/380601/jewish/Soul-Meditation.htm.

Dan, Joseph, and Frank Talmage, eds. *Studies in Jewish Mysticism.* Cambridge, MA: Association for Jewish Studies, 1982.

Davis, F. Hadland. *The Persian Mystics: Wisdom of the East.* London: Murray, 1920.

Dawani, Suheil. Easter message from April 2011. *Bible Lands: Magazine of the Jerusalem and the Middle East Church Association.* (Summer 2011), 23. https://www.jmeca.org.uk.

Douglas-Klotz, Neil. *The Sufi Book of Life: 99 Pathways of the Heart for the Modern Dervish.* New York: Penguin Compass, 2005.

Dyckman, Katherine M., and L. Patrick Carroll. *Inviting the Mystic, Supporting the Prophet: An Introduction to Spiritual Direction.* New York: Paulist, 1981.

Ellis, Marc H. *Revolutionary Forgiveness: Essays on Judaism, Christianity, and the Future of Religious Life.* Waco: Baylor University Press, 2000.

Fleming, Ursula, ed. *Meister Eckhart: The Man from Whom God Hid Nothing.* London: Collins/Fount, 1988.

Ford, David F. and C. C. Pecknold, eds. *The Promise of Scriptural Reasoning.* Malden, MA: Blackwell, 2006.

Frager, Robert, and James Frager, eds. *Essential Sufism.* San Francisco: HarperSanFrancisco, 1997.

Francis, Pope. *Evangelii Gaudium: The Joy of the Gospel.* Dublin: Veritas, 2013.

Freeman, Laurence. "Dangers of the Shallow End." *Church Times*, London, 3 July 2015. https://www.churchtimes.co.uk/articles/2015/3-july/features/features/dangers-of-the-shallow-end.

Freeman, Tzvi. *Bringing Heaven Down to Earth: 365 Meditations from the Wisdom of the Rebbe.* Vancouver, BC: Class One, 2002.

———. "G-d in Your Words." https://www.chabad.org/library/article_cdo/aid/1409035/jewish/Gd-In-Your-Words.htm.

Friends of Mount Athos. *Annual Report 2006.* Oxford: Friends of Mount Athos, 2006.

Gennep, Arnold van. *The Rites of Passage.* Translated by Monika B. Vizedom and Gabrielle L. Caffe. 1909. Reprint, Routledge Library Editions. Anthropology and Ethnography. Religion, Rites & Ceremonies 3. London: Routledge, 2010.

Gikatilla, Joseph ben Abraham. *Gates of Light=Sha'arei Orah.* Translated with an introduction by Avi Weinstein. Sacred Literature Series. New Haven: Yale University Press, 2011.

Green, Arthur, ed. *Jewish Spirituality.* Vol. 2, *From the Sixteenth-Century Revival to the Present.* 2 vols. London: SCM, 1988.

Gregory of Narek. *Speaking with God from the Depths of the Heart: The Lamentations of Gregory of Narek.* Translated by Thomas J. Samuelian. Yerevan, Armenia: Vem, 2017. www.stgregoryofnarek.am.

Gregory of Nyssa. *Ascetical Works.* Translated by Virginia Woods Callahan. Fathers of the Church 58. Washington, DC: Catholic University of America Press, 1967.

Habig, Marion A., ed. *St. Francis of Assisi: Writings and Early Biographies: Omnibus of the Sources for the Life of St Francis.* London: SPCK, 1979.

Helminski, Camille Adams. *Women of Sufism: A Hidden Treasure.* Boulder, CO: Shambhala, 2003.

Hintlian, Kevork. *History of the Armenians in the Holy Land.* Jerusalem: St. James, 1976.

Holy Trinity Monastery. *Prayer Book.* Jordanville, NY: Holy Trinity Monastery, 1960.

Hughes, Gerald W. *God in All Things.* London: Hodder & Stoughton, 2003.

Humphreys, Carolyn. *From Ash to Fire: A Contemporary Journey through the Interior Castle of Teresa of Avila.* New Rochelle, NY: New City, 1992.

Isaac, Bishop of Nineveh. *The Ascetical Homilies.* Translated by Dana Miller. Boston: Holy Transfiguration Monastery, 1984.

———. *The Prayers of Saint Isaac the Syrian.* 2nd ed. Translated by Sebastian Brock. Manton, CA: Divine Ascent, 2011.

Jacobs, Louis, ed. *Jewish Mystical Testimonies.* New York: Schocken, 1977.

Jacobson, Simon. *Toward a Meaningful Life: The Wisdom of Rebbe Menachem Mendel Schneerson.* New York: Morrow, 2004.

Kabbani, Muhammad Hisham. *The Naqshbandi Sufi Tradition Guidebook of Daily Practices and Devotions.* Washington, DC: Islamic Supreme Council of America, 2004.

Kadloubovsky, E., and G. E. H. Palmer, trans. *Writings from the Philokalia on Prayer of the Heart.* London: Faber & Faber, 1977.

Leech, Kenneth. *The Eye of the Storm: Spiritual Resources for the Pursuit of Justice.* London: Darton, Longman & Todd, 1992.

———. *Soul Friend: The Practice of Christian Spirituality.* London: SPCK, 1997.

Lewis, C. S. *The Problem of Pain.* London: Fontana, 1976.

Libreria Editrice Vaticana. *Catechism of the Catholic Church.* London: Chapman, 1994.

Lings, Martin. *What Is Sufism?* Cambridge: Islamic Texts Society, 1993.

Lossky, Vladimir. *The Mystical Theology of the Eastern Church.* London: James Clarke, 1957.

Louth, Andrew. *The Origins of the Christian Mystical Tradition.* 2nd ed. Oxford: Oxford: University Press, 2007.

Maloney, George A. *The Mystic of Fire and Light: St. Symeon the New Theologian.* Denville, NJ: Dimension, 1975.

Mayes, Andrew D. *Beyond the Edge: Spiritual Transitions for Adventurous Souls.* London: SPCK, 2013.

McGinn, Bernard, et al., eds. *Christian Spirituality: Origins to the Twelfth Century.* World Spirituality 16. Christian Spirituality 1. London: SCM, 1985.

Merton, Thomas. *New Seeds of Contemplation.* New York: New Directions, 1961.

Meyendorf, John. *Byzantine Theology.* London: Mowbrays, 1974.

Moses, Paul. *The Saint and the Sultan: The Crusades, Islam and Francis of Assisi's Mission of Peace.* New York: Doubleday Religion, 2009.

Musurillo, Herbert, trans. and ed. *From Glory to Glory: Texts from Gregory of Nyssa's Mystical Writings.* Selected and with an introduction by Jean Daniélou. Crestwood, NY: St Vladimir's Seminary Press, 2001.

Nasr, Seyyed Hossein, ed. *Islamic Spirituality: Manifestations.* World Spirituality 20. London: SCM, 1991.

Nersēs Shnorhali. *Jesus, the Son.* Translated by Mischa Kudian. London: Mashtots, 1986.

———. *Jesus, Son, Only Begotten of the Father: A Prayer.* Translated by Jane S. Wingate. New York: Delphic, 1947.

———. *I Confess with Faith.* Translated by Levon Ounanian. https://shnorhali.com/english.

Nicholson, Reynold A. *The Mystics of Islam.* Khayats Oriental Reprints. Beirut: Khayats, 1966.

Nizami, K. A. "The Naqshbandiyah Order." In *Islamic Spirituality: Manifestations,* edited by Seyyed Hossein Nasr, 162–93. World Spirituality 20. London: SCM, 1991.

Oliver, John W. *Giver of Life: The Holy Spirit in Orthodox Tradition.* A Paraclete Guide. Brewster, MA: Paraclete, 2011.

Ormanian, Malachia. *The Church of Armenia: Her History, Doctrine, Rule, Discipline, Liturgy, Literature, and Existing Condition.* Translated by G. Marcar Gregory. 1912. Reprint, London: Forgotten Books, 2018.

Palmer, George E. H. et al., trans. *The Philokalia.* Vol 2. London: Faber & Faber, 1981.

Peters, F. E. *The Children of Abraham: Judaism, Christianity, Islam.* Princeton Classic Editions. Princeton University Press, 2006.

Peterson, Eugene H. *Christ Plays in Ten Thousand Places: A Conversation in Spiritual Theology.* London: Hodder & Stoughton, 2005.

Plato. *The Republic of Plato.* Translated by Francis Macdonald Cornford. Oxford: Clarendon, 1941.

Prior, Michael, and William Taylor, eds. *Christians in the Holy Land.* London: World of Islam Festival Trust, 1994.

Qalandar, Hamid. *Khair al-majalis.* Delhi: Adabiyat, 2010.

Qleibo, Ali Hussein. *Jerusalem in the Heart.* Jerusalem: Kloreus, 2000.

Rohr, Richard. *The Naked Now: Learning to See as the Mystics See.* New York: Crossroad, 2009.

———. *Everything Belongs: The Gift of Contemplative Prayer.* New York: Crossroad, 2003.

Sarna, Navtej. *Indians at Herod's Gate: A Jerusalem Tale.* New Delhi: Rainlight by Rupa, 2014.

Scholem, Gershom G. *Major Trends in Jewish Mysticism.* London: Thames & Hudson, 1955.

Shannon, William H. *'Something of a Rebel': Thomas Merton, His Life and Works, An Introduction.* Cincinnati: St Anthony Messenger, 1997.

Sheldrake, Phillip. *Images of Holiness: Explorations in Contemporary Spirituality.* London: Darton, Longman & Todd, 1987.

Smith, Paul, trans. *The Book of Baba Farid.* Campbells Creek, Victoria, Australia: New Humanity, 2012.

Star, Jonathan, trans. *Rumi: In the Arms of the Beloved (Praises of God).* New York: Tarcher, 1997.

Symeon, the New Theologian. *The Discourses.* Translated by Carmino J. de Catanzaro. Classics of Western Spirituality. New York: Paulist, 1980.

———. *On the Mystical Life: The Ethical Discourses.* Vol. 2, *On Virtue and Christian Life.* 3 vols. Translated by Alexander Golitzin. New York: St. Vladimir's Seminary Press, 1996.

———. "Three Methods of Attention and Prayer." In *Writings from the Philokalia,* by E. Kadloubovsky, et al., 152–61. London: Faber & Faber, 1977.

———. "You O Christ Are the Kingdom of Heaven." In *Divine Eros: Hymns of St. Symeon the New Theologian.* Translated by Daniel K. Griggs, n.p. Popular Patristics Series 40. Yonkers, NY: St. Vladimir's Seminary Press, 2011.

Teresa of Avila. *The Interior Castle.* Translated by Kieran Kavanaugh and Otilio Rodriguez. Classics of Western Spirituality. New York: Paulist, 1979.

———. *Interior Castle.* Translated by E. Allison Peers. Spiritual Masters. London: Sheed & Ward, 1974.

Third Order Society of St. Francis. "The Principles." *The Third Order Society of St. Francis* (website). https://tssf.org/about-the-third-order/what-is-the-third-order.

United Nations. United Nations Population Fund. "Young People." https://palestine.unfpa.org/en/node/22580.

Tolan, Sandy. *The Lemon Tree.* New York: Black Swan, 2008.

Turner, Victor. *The Ritual Process: Structure and Antistructure.* 1969. Reprint, Piscataway, NJ: Aldine Transaction, 1995.

Turner, Victor, and Deborah Ross. *Image and Pilgrimage in Christian Culture: Anthropological Perspectives.* Lectures on the History of Religions, n.s. 1. New York: Columbia University Press, 1995.

Upton, Charles, trans. *Doorkeeper of the Heart: Versions of Rabi'a.* New York: Pir, 1988.

Vitray-Meyerovitch, Eva de. *Rumi and Sufism.* Translated by Simone Fattal. Sausalito, CA: Post-Apollo, 1987.

Wakefield, Gordon. *A Dictionary of Christian Spirituality.* 3rd ed. London: SCM, 1983.

Wallis, Jim. *The Soul of Politics: A Practical and Prophetic Vision for Change.* Maryknoll, NJ: Orbis, 1994.

Ware, Kallistos. *The Power of the Name: The Jesus Prayer in Orthodox Spirituality.* Oxford: SLG, 1974.

———. *The Inner Kingdom.* New York: St. Vladimir's Seminary Press, 2000.

Williams, Rowan. *The Wound of Knowledge.* 2nd rev. ed. Cambridge, MA: Cowley, 1991.

———. *Teresa of Avila.* London: Continuum, 1991.

Wingate, Andrew. *Celebrating Difference, Staying Faithful: How to Live in a Multi-faith World.* London: Darton, Longman & Todd, 2005.

Wolff, Hans Walter. *Anthropology of the Old Testament.* Translated by Margaret Kohl. Philadelphia: Fortress, 1974.